IMAGES
of America

TAMPA BAY'S
GULF BEACHES
THE FABULOUS 1950S AND 1960S

Pinky Clough, a participant in the Tri-City Suncoast Fiesta, tends to the seagulls in this 1961 promo photo taken on Redington Beach. The Fiesta was an event promoting the area's attractions, hosted jointly by Tampa, St. Petersburg, Clearwater, and the Holiday Isles. (Courtesy of Florida State Archives.)

IMAGES
of America

TAMPA BAY'S GULF BEACHES
THE FABULOUS 1950S AND 1960S

R. Wayne Ayers

ARCADIA
PUBLISHING

Published by Arcadia Publishing
Charleston, South Carolina

Library of Congress Catalog Card Number: 2004104051

For all general information contact Arcadia Publishing at:
Telephone 843-853-2070
Fax 843-853-0044
E-mail sales@arcadiapublishing.com
For customer service and orders:
Toll-Free 1-888-313-2665

Visit us on the Internet at www.arcadiapublishing.com

*This book is dedicated to my wife Nancy, whose creativity, diligent work,
and perseverance have helped make possible yet another chapter in the illustrious
history of our fabulous barrier-island beaches.*

CONTENTS

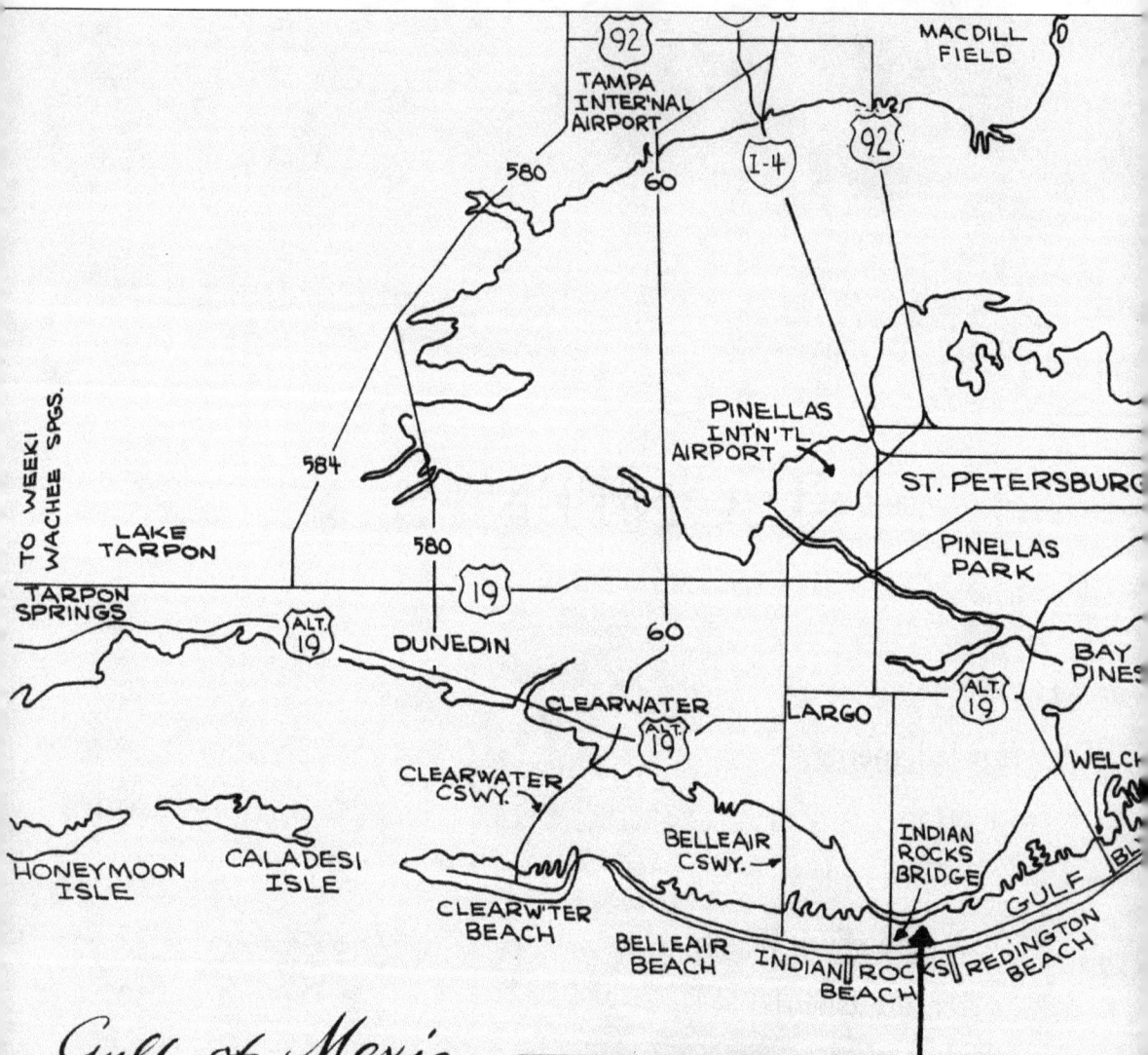

This map of the Tampa Bay region shows the newly created barrier-island beach towns of St. Petersburg Beach, Treasure Island, Madeira Beach, Redington Beach, and Belleair Beach joining the older settlements of Pass-a-Grille, Indian Rocks Beach, and Clearwater Beach.

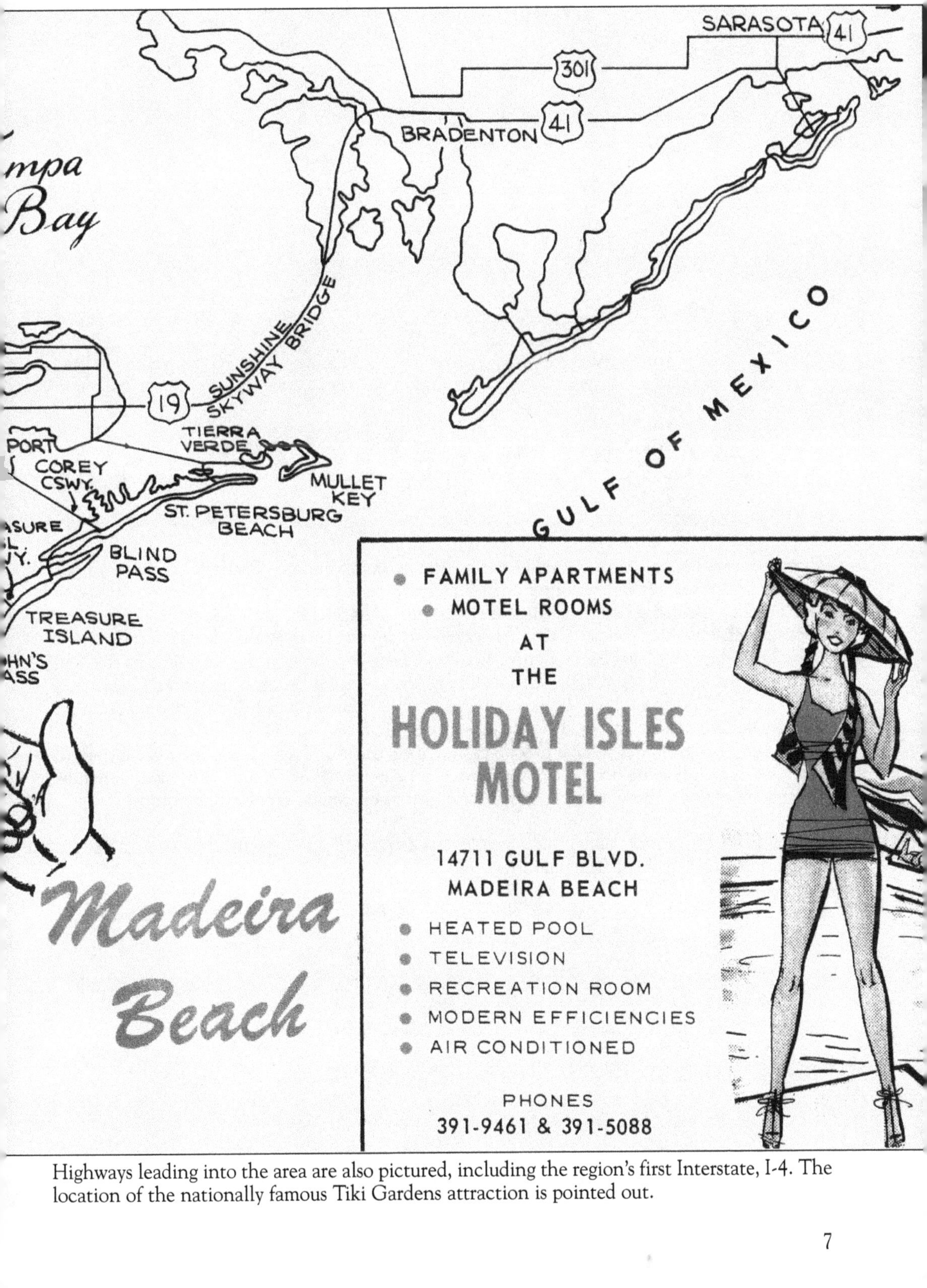
SARASOTA
41
301
BRADENTON
41
Tampa Bay
SUNSHINE SKYWAY BRIDGE
19
TIERRA VERDE
PORT
COREY CSWY.
MULLET KEY
ST. PETERSBURG BEACH
BLIND PASS
TREASURE ISLAND
GULF OF MEXICO
Madeira Beach
FAMILY APARTMENTS
MOTEL ROOMS
AT
THE
HOLIDAY ISLES MOTEL
14711 GULF BLVD.
MADEIRA BEACH
HEATED POOL
TELEVISION
RECREATION ROOM
MODERN EFFICIENCIES
AIR CONDITIONED
PHONES
391-9461 & 391-5088

Highways leading into the area are also pictured, including the region's first Interstate, I-4. The location of the nationally famous Tiki Gardens attraction is pointed out.

ACKNOWLEDGMENTS

The author wishes to thank the following people and organizations for their generous support in providing resources and information that greatly aided me in the creation of this book: The Pinellas County Historical Museum Heritage Village, Jan Luth (director); the Indian Rocks Beach Historical Society, Jan Ockunzzi (president); Alicia Addeo, museum specialist at Heritage Village; Barbara Baker Smith, first volunteer coordinator and organizer of the Gulf Beaches Historical Museum and historian for the Pass-a-Grille Beach Community Church and Pass-a-Grille Woman's Club; Michael Sanders of the Clearwater Historical Society; and Ann Wikoff, archivist at the St. Petersburg Museum of History.

The author consulted a number of sources in writing the introductory sections and captions for this book. The following books and brochures were especially helpful and highly recommended to anyone desiring a more in-depth look at the history of specific beach communities:

Hurley, Frank T. Jr. *Surf, Sand, and Post Card Sunsets: A History of Pass-a-Grille and the Gulf Beaches.* St. Petersburg Beach: Hurley, 1977.

Indian Rocks Beach Area Historical Society. *Indian Rocks: A Pictorial History.* Indian Rocks: Great Outdoors Publishing Company, 1980.

Sanders, Michael L. *Clearwater: A Pictorial History.* Norfolk, VA: Donning Company, 1983.

Shontz, Pat. "50 Years of Madeira in a Minute." Booklet, 1997.

"Sunsational Years: The City of St. Pete Beach Florida 1957–1997." Booklet, 1997.

Williams, Bonnie L. "The Treasure Island Story." Booklet, 2003.

INTRODUCTION

The 1950s and 1960s were an era of transformation for the beaches in the Tampa Bay area. During the decades immediately following World War II, the barrier islands underwent a metamorphosis, changing in a relatively short time from a collection of sleepy hamlets into a booming vacation mecca.

Part of the catalyst for this change was the war itself. During World War II, many service personnel were stationed in Florida before being sent overseas. The warm climate proved ideal for training exercises, and tourist accommodations, especially the bigger hotels, could be requisitioned by the government and offered perfect housing facilities for the troops.

Along the Tampa Bay area beaches, the Don CeSar at Pass-a-Grille and the Belleview Biltmore at Clearwater housed large numbers of military personnel. The servicemen evidently liked what they saw of the area, and after the war, thousands of ex-G.I.s enjoying newfound prosperity packed their newly minted families into their automobiles and began a sojourn to enjoy the Florida sun. A much improved road system of direct, well-paved highways dotted with roadside attractions made getting there part of the fun, rather than the dicey proposition of pre-war years. The concept of an extended vacation for middle-class America was born, and the miles of pristine Gulf beaches in the Tampa Bay area were a main beneficiary.

Previously undeveloped beach areas from Pass-a-Grille to Clearwater began to fill in with motels, a newly evolved accommodation featuring amenities such as curbside parking, TV, air conditioning, and swimming pools, which fit the bill perfectly for these newly mobile families. Even older properties willing to invest in a new paint job or put up a TV aerial gained a new lease on life as surging demand for "a place to stay" brought a general prosperity to the area.

Family oriented attractions such as roadside zoos, aquariums, gardens, deep-sea fishing, and miniature golf (called putt-putt golf) joined the main event—beach related activities—to give vacationing families a full, bordering on exhaustive, measure of fun in the sun. Almost overnight the beaches were transformed from a sparsely populated, semi-wilderness area viewed mostly as fishing grounds and a tourist curiosity into a family playground for a burgeoning middle-class society that had largely stayed close to home prior to the war.

It was during this post-war era of the 1950s and 1960s that the beach communities we know today were incorporated and developed. Swift change engulfed the barrier islands during this period, and a new era of prosperity, which has never since slowed or abated, was born.

The only losers in this newfound prosperity, besides the natural beach environment, were the big hotels located mostly on the mainland, which had catered mainly to wealthy wintering socialites. Even the beachfront Don CeSar was viewed as a monstrosity unable to compete in an age dominated by automobile-oriented tourists seeking family amenities. The Don survived for a while as offices for the Veterans Administration before closing up in 1969. Rehabilitation of the Don would have to wait until luxury and service again became fashionable in the jet-age 1970s.

Pass-a-Grille, at the southern tip of the barrier-island strip, is the only community to have largely preserved its pre-war character and appearance. Its downtown section along Eighth Avenue looks much the same, even today, as it did during the early 1900s. Many of the area's original cottages have been restored and dot the streets of the Historic District. Pass-a-Grille, though a part of St. Petersburg Beach since the mid-1950s, has mostly resisted the development surges that have made over the barrier-island communities to the north. Even during the tourist boom of the 1950s, Pass-a-Grille continued to rely on 1920s-era accommodations such as the Pass-a-Grille Hotel.

St. Petersburg Beach, now St. Pete Beach, was created on July 9, 1957, after a joint referendum to combine the municipalities of Pass-a-Grille, St. Petersburg Beach, Don CeSar Place, Belle Vista Beach, and an unincorporated area passed by a five-vote margin. Pass-a-Grille and St. Petersburg Beach voted heavily against the consolidation, while the smaller communities provided the margin of victory.

Although Pass-a-Grille was largely built out by the 1920s, the areas to the north remained mostly undeveloped until the post-war years. The Don CeSar stood in relative isolation for years, being converted to Veterans Administration offices at the beginning of the development era following World War II.

The new city of St. Petersburg Beach was soon caught up in the beach development boom, and the ex-G.I.s and their families who returned to find their old Don CeSar home off limits found an array of shiny new art-deco motel properties ready to accommodate them. The Corey Avenue business district was laid out in the late 1930s and became the main street of the thriving community.

Two popular "Old Florida" attractions were also located on St. Petersburg Beach: the Aquatarium and the London Wax Museum. The Aquatarium featured marine aquariums and dolphin shows under a giant geodesic dome. The attraction opened in 1964 and thrived during its early years, employing over 120 workers at its peak.

Further north along the barrier islands, the city of **Treasure Island** was created on May 3, 1955, from the consolidation of the towns of Sunset Beach, Boca Ciega, Treasure Island, and Sunshine Beach. Developers soon added to that acreage with the creation of the Isle of Capri, Isle of Palms, and Paradise Island from Intracoastal landfills.

Construction of the art-deco landmark Sands Motel in 1948 began a motel building frenzy to accommodate the hordes of tourists who descended on the barrier island during the post-war boom days. By the mid-1950s, the Treasure Island beachfront was lined wall-to-wall with rows of sparkling motels, and visitors entering the city emerged from the Australian pine–lined bridge from the mainland to be greeted by a sea of beckoning neon and glitz. The Thunderbird, from its commanding position at the foot of the causeway, became a symbol of one of the nation's hottest vacation spots. The art-deco shopping district created at the intersection of the causeway and Gulf Boulevard across from the T-Bird became the center of Treasure Island commercial activity and featured shops offering "unusual gifts and jewelry from around the world to authentic Florida crafts." Promotional brochures of the era touted Treasure Island as the "Land of High Adventure and Heart of the Holiday Isles."

One of the first beach communities to incorporate in the wake of the post-war boom was **Madeira Beach**, which officially became a town on May 5, 1947. At the time of incorporation, about 1,000 building lots were available within the approximately one-square-mile town borders, which ran from 140th Avenue to 155th Avenue. Madeira Beach's main street was Gulf Boulevard, and businesses were opened along both sides of the thoroughfare north and south from the causeway.

A few small hotels and motels dotted the beachfront, but single-family home development dominated in Madeira Beach until the condo age hit in the 1970s and 1980s. Aerial photos of the area taken even as late at the 1960s show a beachfront lined mostly with homes. Dredging began in the 1950s to create the Harbor Drive neighborhood and other bay-front residential communities.

In 1951, the town of Madeira Beach merged with South Madeira, creating the city of Madeira Beach with new boundaries extending to John's Pass. Additional annexations along the Welch Causeway gave the newly formed city room for an elementary school and a new shopping center to be anchored, as today, by a Publix Supermarket. Beach erosion, which threatened to strip away much of the city's most vital asset, was stemmed in the late 1950s by the installation of 37 concrete groins, each 200 feet long, at 200–300-foot intervals along the Gulf. The opening of the new Madeira Beach Causeway in 1962 brought another population surge to the area, and Madeira Beach, along with the other barrier-island communities, rode out the 1950s and 1960s on a wave of growth and prosperity.

The area that came be known as the **Redingtons** grew around the Tides Hotel, the famed beach resort built in the mid-1930s by real estate developer Charles Redington to draw development to a mostly deserted stretch of beach. The gambit was a success. Settlement of the area followed the coming of the Tides, the first major development on the beaches since the building of the Don CeSar in 1926.

The town of **Redington Beach** was created in 1944 shortly after World War II. The landmark Tides hit its heyday in the 1950s and 1960s, drawing tourists from all over and hosting famous celebrities of the day, from Marilyn Monroe and Joe DiMaggio to Ronald Reagan. The Tides Bath Club, for years the only private club in southern Pinellas County, became the social center of the beaches.

Population in the area boomed in the mid-1950s as motels sprang up to feed off the Tides's success, and new subdivisions drew both seasonal and permanent residents to the prime waterfront location right in the middle of the barrier-island beach strip.

The 1950s population surge resulted in the formation of two more Redingtons, **North Redington Beach** in 1953 and **Redington Shores** in 1955, from parts of the original Redington Beach. Redington Beach developed as a community of single-family homes, while North Redington Beach and Redington Shores featured the more typical mix of residential, commercial, and later high-rise condos along the beachfront. The continued prosperity of the Tides and the adjacent communities bearing his name served as a glowing testament to the vision and foresight of real estate magnate Charles E. Redington.

Indian Rocks, a loosely defined area since its ill-fated attempt at incorporation in the 1920s, made a second try, which took, in 1955. With roots going back to the 1800s, Indian Rocks—along with Pass-a-Grille and Clearwater Beach—was one of the original beach settlements. The Indian Rocks area included today's Indian Shores as well as Belleair Beach and Belleair Shore on the barrier island and parts of Largo on the mainland side of the Intracoastal Waterway.

The present boundaries of Indian Rocks Beach were set in the 1955 incorporation. Already an established community that had witnessed a real estate boom in the 1920s, Indian Rocks Beach underwent another population surge following World War II. This surge saw the development of businesses along the east side of Gulf Boulevard and residential neighborhoods formed from the dredging of the Intracoastal.

During the 1950s and 1960s a number of the original beach cottages formerly occupied as vacation retreats by Tampans were converted to residences lived in year-round or during the winter season by snowbirds. The mid-century population boom did not substantially alter the original eclectic cottage character of Indian Rocks Beach. Only the addition of businesses established along Gulf Boulevard and the construction of ranch-style homes on the newly dredged "fingers" of land altered the look of the city in any great fashion from its pre-war appearance. Of course, the coming of the condos in the 1970s and 1980s brought great change to the beachfront, but a number of the earlier cottage-style homes and tourist accommodations can still be found, even on the west side of the boulevard.

Indian Rocks Beach South Shore, which had been considered a part of the unincorporated Indian Rocks area since the early days, incorporated as a separate town in 1949. The land included the area known as the Narrows, where the old bridge to the mainland was located, south to the Redingtons. In 1973, the town was renamed **Indian Shores**.

Indian Shores was home to **Tiki Gardens**, the nationally renowned Old Florida attraction created in the early 1960s by Frank and Jo Byars as an outgrowth of their Polynesian-themed Signal House gift shop. The gardens grew during the 1960s and 1970s to a 12-acre Polynesian paradise, featuring jungle trails filled with exotic plants and animals, towered over by the park's signature giant tikis.

Belleair Beach emerged from a largely undeveloped area that served as a target range for World War II Air Force bombers to become a prime target for residential development following the war. Round-the-clock dredging of the Intracoastal Waterway began shortly after the war and continued into the 1950s. This operation created the fingers of land that were divided into the hundreds of residential lots that were to define the future character of Belleair Beach. The opening of the Belleair Beach Causeway bridge in 1950 brought an influx of new residents to the area and spurred a home-building frenzy that filled in the newly created sand lots with sparkling white-washed ranch-style dwellings. The city of Belleair Beach was incorporated on March 16, 1950, and began its emergence as an almost exclusively residential neighborhood, with no commercial enterprises save a scattering of motels along the beachfront. This city's residential character has been maintained through the years, supplemented by low-rise condo development on the west side of Gulf Boulevard during the 1970s and 1980s.

Incorporation of **Belleair Shore** came about in 1955, when owners of beachfront property sought to carve out a separate identity with a somewhat more exclusive appeal. Development was strictly limited to single-family dwellings. Spacious one-story homes with lushly landscaped grounds became the signature of the upscale enclave. Today, the original structures are being replaced with multi-story mansions, setting a new standard of exclusivity.

North of Belleair Beach, the spit of land known as **Sand Key**—actually Sand Key is the entire barrier island south to where the Park Boulevard bridge is now—remained undeveloped and in a semi-primitive state throughout the 1950s and 1960s. Except for the few beach cabanas maintained for guests by the Belleview Biltmore Hotel, the area retained its wilderness character until the city of Clearwater sold the tract for development in the 1980s. Today, a parcel at the northern tip of Sand Key is maintained as a county park and beach parking area.

Clearwater Beach, which had seen some development in the early 1900s as a resort area of the city of Clearwater, received a major boost from the post-war tourist boom. Touted during the 1950s as the "World's Safest Beach" due to its gentle slope into the Gulf, the area drew large numbers of family vacationers seeking modest accommodations and summertime fun. Clearwater Beach emerged during the 1950s and 1960s from a sleepy beach town anchored by the sprawling Clearwater Beach Hotel and a few scattered tourist amenities to become a resort powerhouse. Scores of mom-and-pop motels were built to accommodate the post-war wave of vacationing families.

Extension and development of the Pier 60 complex in 1962 gave the area a focal point and became the entryway for visitors to enjoy the wide and extensive public beach that stretched out on both sides. The opening of the Clearwater Pass bridge in 1962 gave visitors unbroken access to the string of Gulf beaches from Clearwater to Pass-a-Grille.

From St. Petersburg Beach at the south end to Clearwater Beach at the northern edge, Americans on vacation flocked to the barrier islands that make up Tampa Bay's Gulf beaches. The beaches, the people who visited them, and the accommodations and attractions that sprang up to house and entertain the tourists and their families make up the fabric of an era that will long be fondly remembered.

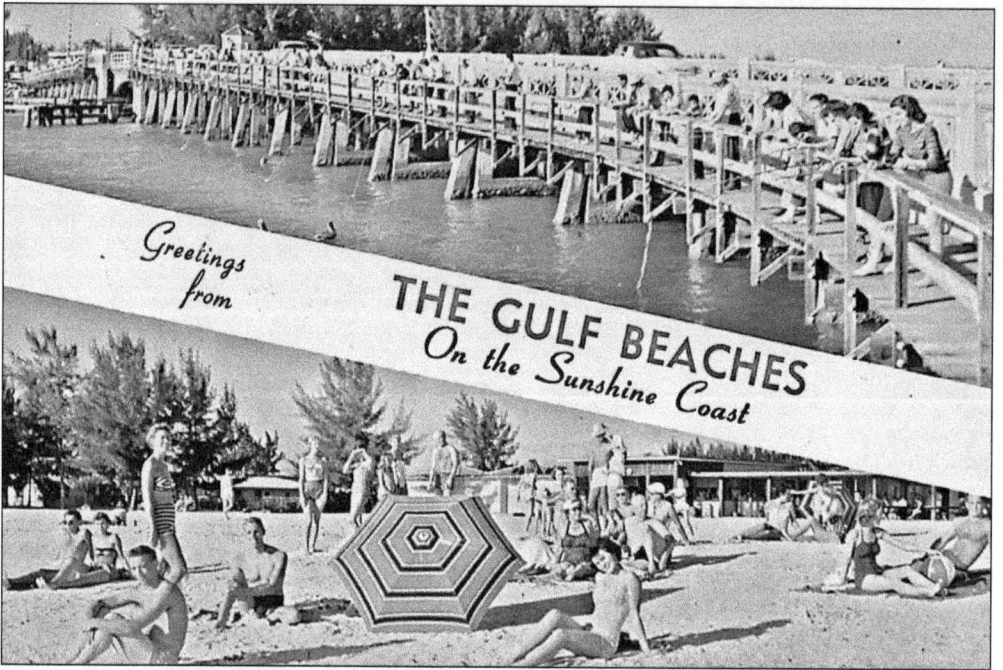

Greetings from

THE GULF BEACHES
On the Sunshine Coast

Tampa Bay's Gulf beaches in the 1950s and 1960s offered great fishing, either in deep-sea boats or from the area's many fine piers and bridges . . . and of course, miles of seashore sparkling in the ever-present Florida sun.

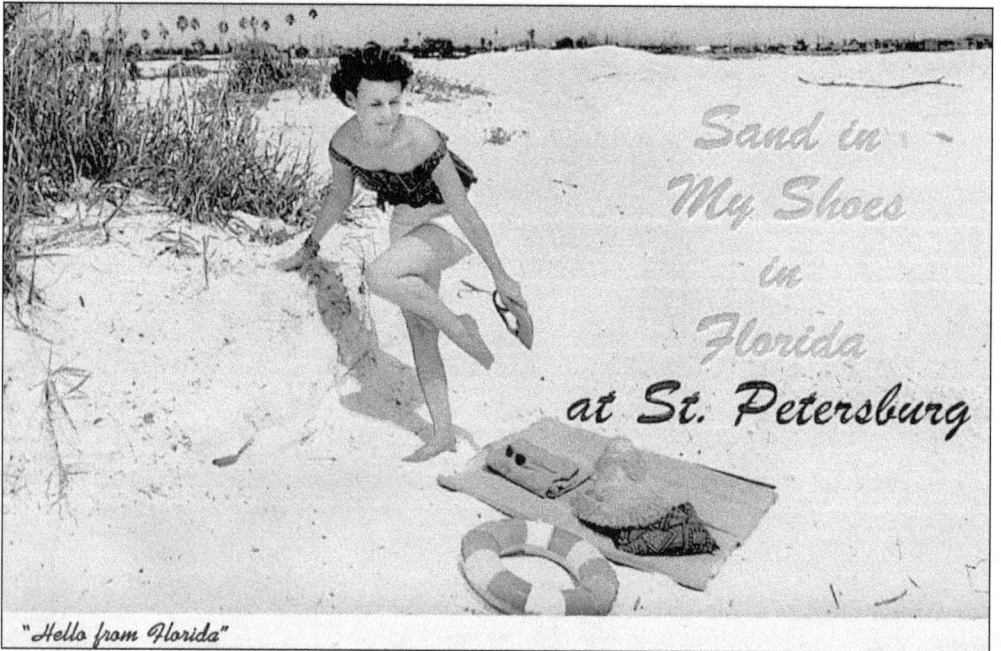

Sand in
My Shoes
in
Florida
at St. Petersburg

"Hello from Florida"

One

PASS-A-GRILLE

Pass-A-Grill Beach, Florida

This aerial view of Pass-a-Grille, which in 1957 became part of the city of St. Petersburg Beach, shows a nearly filled-in community. As the oldest settlement along the beach, Pass-a-Grille, located at the south end of the beach strip, has maintained and preserved many of its original commercial buildings and dwellings. The structure jutting into the beach in the right foreground is the Pass-a-Grille Beach Hotel, which was the Pass-a-Grille Casino in the 1920s.

This photo, taken before the freeze of 1962, and the one to the right, taken after the freeze, show how the cold temperatures wiped out Pass-a-Grille's ubiquitous Australian pines, which had become the dominant vegetation in the area following its introduction as an exotic species in the 1920s. Note how erosion has nearly erased the beach along the Gulf.

The Pass-a-Grille Beach Hotel, formerly the Pass-a-Grille Casino, was Pass-a-Grille's largest hostelry during the post-war years. The hotel served guests year-round until it was demolished following a devastating fire in 1967.

Pass-A-Grille Beach Hotel - Pass-A-Grille Beach, Fla.   2-G-305

This view shows Pass-a-Grille denuded of pines. A jetty built in 1959–1960 and extended in 1962 has facilitated the natural buildup of sand, creating a wide beach.

The hotel's mid-peninsula beachfront location made it a popular vacation destination.

Pass-A-Grille Beach, Florida — Pass-A-Grille Hotel in Background   C132

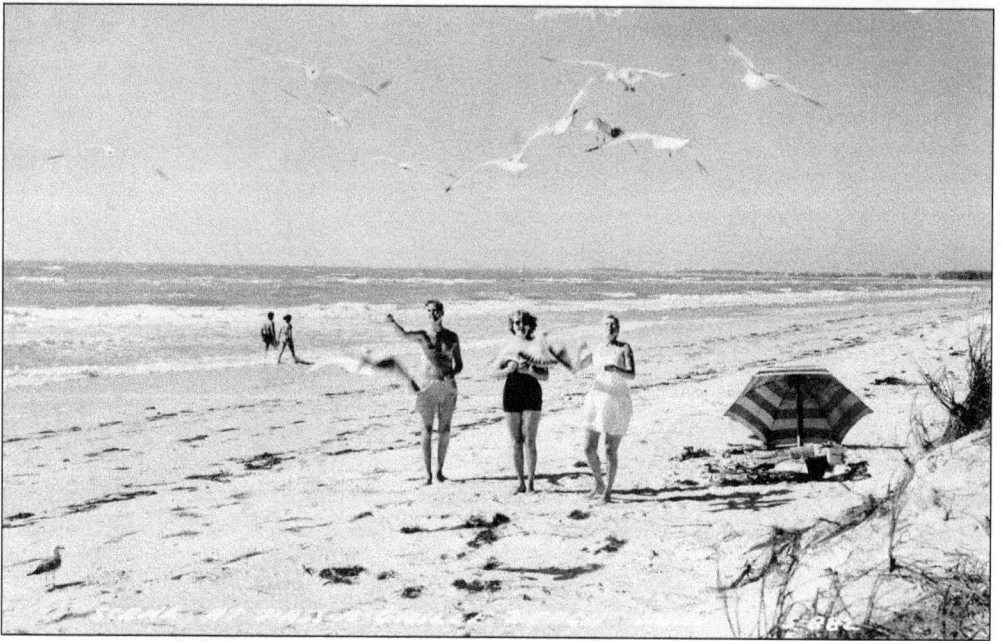

Pass-a-Grille's wide sandy beaches, largely the result of the jetty constructed at the south end of the peninsula in the early 1960s, offer plenty of opportunity for strolling and engaging the flocks of seabirds.

S-80—Colorful Pass-a-Grille Beach, Florida "on the Gulf of Mexico"

This view shows the beachside table service available at the Pass-a-Grille Beach Hotel.

This aerial view shows the downtown area (left), the Pass-a-Grille Beach Hotel (upper center), and the docks along the bay.

Pass - A - Grille Beach, Florida   Air Photo by Tom Brown

This beach view from the late 1960s looking north shows the site (foreground) of the former Pass-a-Grille Beach Hotel, now occupied by a beach pavilion.

Fishing off the Docks at Pass-A-Grill, Fla.

Captain Wilson Hubbard arrived in Pass-a-Grille in 1929 and began catching and selling fish from the Merry Pier. His purchase of five rowboats and 40 cane poles when he was 17 was the beginning of what became the famed Hubbard's marina operation. Hubbard bought his first charter boat after World War II, and the Eighth Avenue Pier became known as Hubbard's Pier.

Municipal Dock Scene-Pass-A-Grille Beach, Fla.   2-G-306

This c. 1950 photo gives an early view of Hubbard's operation on the municipal dock.

Hubbard expanded and enhanced his fishing operation during the 1950s and 1960s, offering the first half-day fishing party in 1954 and an 18-hour fishing trip beginning in 1956. In the mid-1970s, Captain Hubbard moved his operation to John's Pass.

Anglers of all ages, male and female, try their luck at the 1964 Fishathon, sponsored by the Pass-a-Grille Yacht Club. (Courtesy of Heritage Village.)

Pass-a-Grille Way offers a pleasant waterfront drive along the Boca Ciega Bay.

The service businesses shown here on Eighth Avenue have given way in recent years to upscale art galleries and boutiques. This scene looks east to Hubbard's Pier.

The Neptune Grille, at Twentieth Avenue and Pass-a-Grille Way, offered seafood along with a typical 1950s menu of steaks, chops, and chicken. The eatery advertised a dining experience "Where every meal is a memory."

S-147—Pass-a-Grille Way
Showing
Sekon-in-the-Palms Hotel
Pass-a-Grille Beach, Florida

Tourist accommodations included the Sekon in the Palms Hotel and Cottages, which featured a location "30 seconds from the beach" and an orchestra that played nightly for dinner and concerts. Owner Ralph Dellevie also operated Sekon Lodge in Upper Saranac Lake, New York. The message on the card, curiously, reads, "Greetings from the land of plenty—loads of roast beef."

S-146—Cameo Apartments, One of the Many Fine Hostelries on the Greater Gulf Beaches. Pass-A-Grille Beach, Fla.

OC-H1396

The Cameo Apartments offered visitors a residential setting with beach access across Gulf Way. The structure, at Eighteenth Avenue, now houses the Camelot by the Sea Apartments.

This group enjoys a frolic along the beach near the Don CeSar Hotel, which can be seen in the background. (Courtesy of St. Petersburg Museum of History.)

24

Two

ST. PETERSBURG BEACH

St. Petersburg Beach, at the southern end of the barrier-island strip, featured miles of white sandy beaches and a pair of popular attractions, the London Wax Museum and the Aquatarium marine-dolphin exhibit. The city was created in 1957 from a consolidation of the Long Key municipalities of Pass-a-Grille, St. Petersburg Beach, Don CeSar Place, Belle Vista Beach, and an unincorporated area. The merger passed by only five votes in a joint referendum held July 9, 1957.

This 1952 view of downtown St. Petersburg Beach shows the old Corey Causeway bridge. Results of the post-war development boom are evident, with very few vacant lots visible amid the densely packed development. (Courtesy of Heritage Village.)

By 1960, the Bay Islands created in Boca Ciega Bay allowed construction of a new shorter bridge from the mainland. In this view, both the old and new bridges can be seen. Note that St. Petersburg Beach is now almost totally developed.

By the late 1940s and early 1950s, dredging operations were underway up and down the barrier islands, creating new fingers of waterfront land in Boca Ciega Bay for residential development. This 1952 aerial photo looking north shows the new developments of Don CeSar Place and Belle Vista, which became a part of St. Petersburg Beach following the 1957 consolidation. At the time of this photo, the mangrove island known as Mud Key (lower right) was still undeveloped. (Courtesy of Heritage Village.)

This 1960 view shows Don CeSar Place well developed as a community of ranch-style homes by this time, while swampy Mud Key has become Vina del Mar Island. Standing prominently in the background is the Don CeSar Hotel, which gradually deteriorated during the 1950s and 1960s when it was used as offices for the Veterans Administration. (Courtesy of Florida State Archives.)

The early 1950s saw new development occurring wherever vacant parcels of land were available. Just south of the pass along the beach is the extensive Gulf Winds Apartment complex. (Courtesy of Heritage Village.)

The Gulf Winds Apartments and Villas were touted in 1952 as "one of the most ambitious recent building projects." The six-building project offered 326 apartments and villas and was described in the accompanying ad as "the largest apartment colony of its kind on Florida's Gulf Coast." It included the Imperial House Restaurant, operated by Morrison's Cafeterias. The development has survived subsequent beachfront makeovers and is today the Gulf Winds Resort Condominiums. (Courtesy of Heritage Village.)

S. 65—Sun and Surf Bathing Along St. Petersburg,
Florida's Beautiful Gulf Beaches

Two-piece bathing suits became popular after the war, when more relaxed dress standards allowed women to show their midriffs.

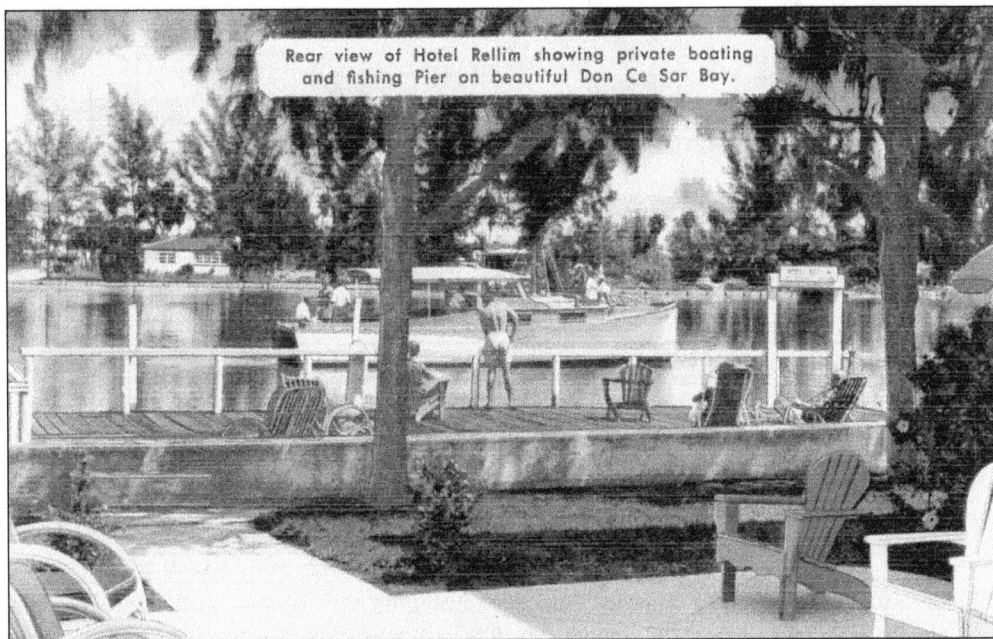

Rear view of Hotel Rellim showing private boating and fishing Pier on beautiful Don Ce Sar Bay.

The Hotel Rellim, which fronted the bay near the Don CeSar, catered to Jewish guests during an era when ethnic and racial minorities were denied admittance to many accommodations.

Your Television Guide

WSUN — CHANNEL 38
All Times Listed P.M.

SUNDAY	MONDAY	TUESDAY
6:00 Men ot Annap.	6:00 Captain Mac	6:30 Conflict
6:30 Hollywood Film	6:30 Wire Service	7:30 Wyatt Earp
8:00 Compass	7:30 Bold Journey	8:00 Broken Arrow
8:30 Hayride	8:00 A.B.C. Presents	8:30 Telephone Time
9:00 Mike Wallace	8:30 Lawrence Welk	9:00 Polka Time
9:30 News-weather	9:30 O'Henry	9:30 Stage 7
9:45 Film	10:00 Suncoast Byline	10:00 Suncoast Byline
11:00 News-Weather	10:30 Film	10:30 Film
11:15 Confident. File		

WEDNESDAY	THURSDAY	FRIDAY	SATURDAY
6:00 Captain Mac	6:30 Superman	6:00 Capt. Mac	6:00 Sherlock Holms
6:30 Disneyland	7:00 Cartoon Carn'vl	6:35 Rin Tin Tin	6:30 Flight No. 7
7:30 Navy Log	7:30 Waterfront	7:00 Jim Bowie	7:00 Billy Graham
8:00 Ozzie-Harriet	8:00 Theatre Time	7:30 Crossroads	7:30 T.B.A.
8:30 Ford Theatre	9:00 Focus	8:00 Key Club Play.	8:00 Lawrence Welk
9:00 Fights	9:30 Liberace	8:30 Wst'rn Marshal	9:00 Country Music
9:45 Great Fights	10:00 Suncoast Byline	9:00 Date/Angels	9:30 Gildersleeve
10:00 Suncoast Byline	10:30 Film	9:30 Badge 714	10:00 My Hero
10:30 Film		10:00 Suncoast Byline	10:45 Film
		10:30 Film	

WTVT — CHANNEL 13
All Times Listed P.M.

SUNDAY	MONDAY	TUESDAY
6:00 Lassie	7:00 Robin Hood	7:00 Phil Silvers
6:30 Favorite Husb.	7:30 Godfrey	7:30 Private Sec'y.
7:00 Ed Sullivan	8:00 Whiting Girls	8:00 To Tell Truth
8:00 GE Theatre	8:30 Richard ◇	8:30 Spotlite Thea.
8:30 Hitchcock	9:00 Studio One	9:00 $64,000 ?
9:00 $64,000 Chal'ng	10:00 State Trooper	9:30 Dr. Hudson
9:30 What's My Line	10:30 Cross Current	10:00 Cochise Sheriff
10:00 Soldier Fortune	11:00 News—Film	10:30 Jimmy Dean
10:30 News		

WEDNESDAY	THURSDAY	FRIDAY	SATURDAY
7:00 Vic Damone	7:00 Sgt. Preston	7:00 West Point	7:00 Jimmy Durante
8:00 The Millionaire	7:30 Climax	7:30 Destiny	7:30 2 for the Money
8:30 I've Got Secret	8:30 Playhouse 90	8:00 Mr. Adams	8:00 Gale Storm
9:00 20th Cent. Fox	10:00 Name that Tune	8:30 Schlitz	8:30 S.R.O. Playhse
10:00 Martin Kane	10:30 Bob Cummings	9:00 Under Current	9:00 Gunsmoke
10:30 Starlite Playhse	11:00 News	9:30 Pantomine Quiz	9:30 Crusade
11:00 News	11:15 Sports	10:00 Whirly Birds	10:00 Burns & Allen
11:30 Film	11:30 Film	10:30 Beat the Clock	10:45 Best Hollywood
		11:00 News—Film	

WFLA — CHANNEL 8
All Times Listed P.M.

SUNDAY	MONDAY	TUESDAY
6:30 Circus Boy	7:00 Sir Lancelot	6:30 Fla. Headlines
7:00 Steve Allen	7:30 Action to Night	7:00 Arthur Murray
8:00 T.V. Playhouse	8:00 Twenty-one	7:30 Panic
9:00 The Web	8:30 Arthur Murray	8:00 Meet McGraw
9:30 People R Funny	9:00 Ted Mack	8:30 Summer Show
10:00 Premier Thea.	9:30 Howard Prsnts	9:00 Nat King Cole
11:00 Film	10:00 Death Valley	9:30 Wrestling
	10:30 Night Desk	10:00 Public Defender
	11:00 Film	10:30 Night Desk
		11:00 Film

WEDNESDAY	THURSDAY	FRIDAY	SATURDAY
6:30 Fla. Healines	6:45 NBC News	6:45 NBC News	7:00 J. La Rosa
7:00 Readers Digest	7:00 Best of Groucho	7:00 Blondie	8:00 Mystery Riders
7:30 FatherKnows	7:30 Dragnet	7:30 of Riley	8:30 Dollar a Second
8:00 Television Thea	8:00 People's Choice	8:00 On Trial	9:00 Geo. Gobel
9:00 This' Your Life	8:30 Hgh-Low	8:30 Big Moment	9:30 Adventure
9:30 Masquerade	9:00 Video Theatre	9:00 Fights	10:00 Night Desk
10:00 Monte Cristo	10:00 Hiway Patrol	10:00 Howard Prsnts	10:15 Grand Ole Opry
10:30 Night Desk	10:30 Night Desk	10:30 Night Desk	
11:00 Film	11:00 Film		

TV was a sought-after tourist amenity, especially during its novelty stage in the early to mid-1950s. This 1957 schedule of the Tampa Bay area's three television channels features classic favorites such as *Ozzie and Harriett*, *Gunsmoke*, *Dragnet*, *The Ed Sullivan Show*, and the popular *$64,000 Question* quiz program.

Drive-in movies were a favorite form of entertainment for vacationing families. The Sky Vue Drive-In Theater was located just across the Corey Causeway, convenient to St. Petersburg Beach and Treasure Island. The Sky Vue charged a 60¢ admission, kids free, to see features playing in the summer of 1957.

St. Petersburg Beach's fledgling downtown along Corey Avenue was a busy emporium in the 1950s, offering tourist-related services and typical businesses of the era. A market, movie theater, bar, beach sundries, and menswear store can be spotted in this scene.

The Corey Avenue commercial district was laid out and developed in the late 1930s by realtor William Upham. By the early 1950s, the street was bustling with business. Today, the avenue remains the thriving hub of downtown St. Pete Beach. (Courtesy of Heritage Village.)

Fueled by prosperity and the area's rapid growth, banks grew phenomenally during the 1950s and 1960s. The crowds of customers waiting at the Gulf Beach Bank at St. Petersburg Beach were a testament to a booming economy. Beach residents enjoyed the convenience of having a bank right in town, rather than going to St. Petersburg to cash their checks. (Courtesy of Heritage Village.)

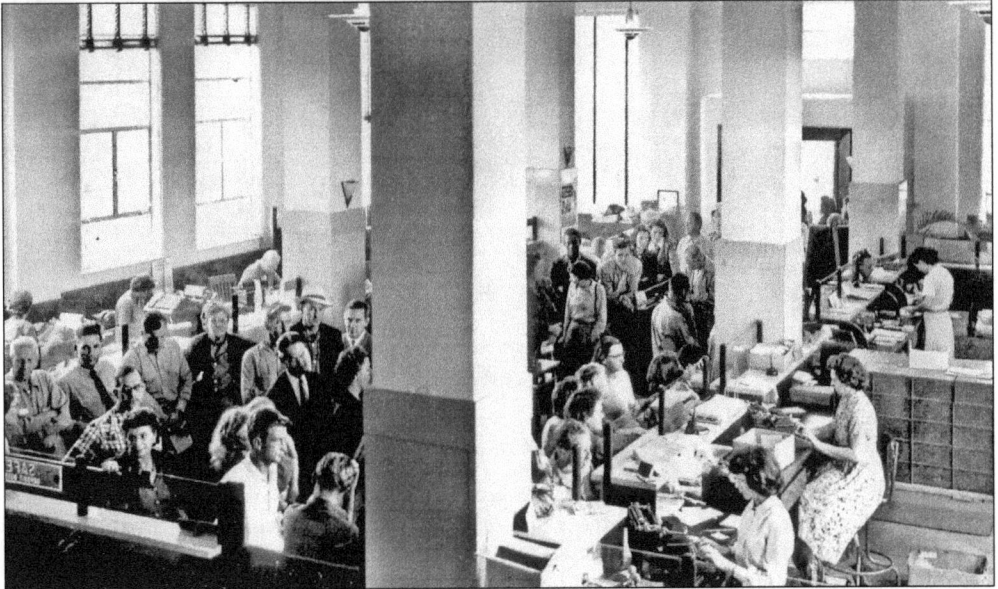

London Wax Museum, St. Petersburg Beach, Florida

St. Petersburg Beach was home to two major "Old Florida" attractions, the London Wax Museum and the Aquatarium. The Wax Museum was part of a chain operation associated with the renowned Madame Tussaud's Museum in London. The museum was owned by Ted Stambaugh and was located on the site of the current Silas Dent's Restaurant at 5505 Gulf Boulevard, run by Rob and Debbie Stambaugh.

Inside the museum, visitors encountered "more than 100 famous characters in the present and past" in wax depictions described as so realistic "they seem alive." This scene from the St. Petersburg Beach museum features Jose Gaspar and other pirates of Gasparilla fame.

The Aquatarium, with its futuristic geodesic dome, opened to great fanfare in 1964 at St. Petersburg Beach. The 18-acre attraction featured marine exhibits and dolphin acts, and drew large crowds during the 1960s. Competition from the Disney megaparks and Busch Gardens resulted in the decline of smaller venues like the Aquatarium, and the park closed in 1978.

"Thor," one of the Aquatarium's educated porpoises likes traveling in the "best circles."

The multi-million dollar AQUATARIUM, located just off Gulf Boulevard, St. Petersburg Beach, is the world's largest marine attraction. The 18-acre complex includes the main aquaria tank of 1-1/4 million gallons, a performance training tank under the Golden Dome, and 34 individual reef tanks. Educated porpoises and sea lions entertain with special acts, climaxed by hand-to-hand underwater feeding of the specimens by a pretty staff diver. Shows are presented every hour, daily.

THE WORLD'S LARGEST
MARINE SHOW!
ST. PETERSBURG BEACH, FLORIDA
ON THE GULF OF MEXICO AT 67 AVENUE

aquatarium

The attraction was heavily promoted during its tenure, but in the end its advertising budget could not compete with the millions spent by Disney and Busch.

Aerial view of the crowds at the Aquatarium

Crowds gather to watch a dolphin show at the exhibit's main tank, which was billed as the world's largest and described as 3.5 stories high and holding 1.24 million gallons of seawater.

A "double jump" was one of the featured acts at Aquatarium shows.

Aquatarium - St. Petersburg Beach, Florida

Visitors on the left watch the dolphins and sea lions through 120 viewing windows that surround the main tank on two levels. On the right are reef garden exhibits.

The geodesic dome housed a smaller training tank and also featured animal acts.

Thor the Dolphin takes a fish from his trainer's mouth during a performance under the Golden Dome.

Performing sea lions display their talents at an Aquatarium show.

Performing Sea Lions at the Aquatarium

Three

TREASURE ISLAND

Treasure Island, created in 1955 with the consolidation of the towns of Sunset Beach, Boca Ciega, Treasure Island, and Sunshine Beach, quickly gained popularity as a tourist hot spot. Visitors were greeted upon arrival over the causeway by the landmark Thunderbird, an appropriate introduction to a beachfront lined with snazzy new art-deco motels. The T-Bird still stands at the foot of the Treasure Island Causeway as an enduring symbol of the city's commitment to tourism and historic preservation.

Completion of the Treasure Island Causeway in 1939 gave motorists easy access to the beaches and facilitated the area's emergence as a center for tourism following the war.

Development in the area was slow to begin despite the opening of the causeway. This 1941 view shows (1) Causeway Isles, (2) Treasure Island Causeway Bridge, (3) Isle of Palms, (4) Isle of Capri, and (5) Sunshine Beach. The large mangrove islands in the foreground became Paradise Isle. (Courtesy of Heritage Village.)

The Sands, built in 1948, was the first modern motel to be constructed on Treasure Island. Featuring drive-up accommodations, spacious grounds, and rooms that offered every guest at least a peek at the Gulf, the property quickly gained popularity and became a prototype for the scores of similar structures that were to follow. The Sands still stands as a beachfront icon at 11800 Gulf Boulevard. (Courtesy of Heritage Village.)

Beachfront property values were still relatively low during the beaches' discovery years, giving developers the opportunity to include spacious grounds even in more modest properties like the Catalina. The motel, located at 11440 Gulf Boulevard, is now called Trails End.

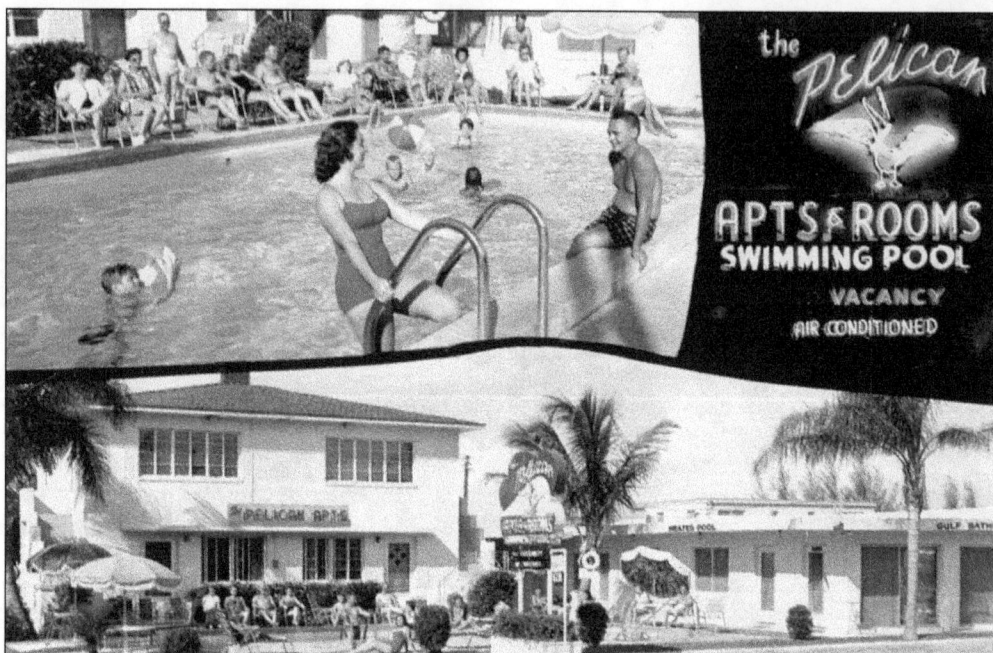

Located across the road from the Sands, the Pelican was typical of the smaller modest apartment motels that appealed to vacationing families. The Pelican offered lower rates than Gulf-front properties but still featured sought-after amenities, such as a swimming pool, air conditioning, and TV. The Pelican is now the Roadside Inn, located at 11799 Gulf Boulevard.

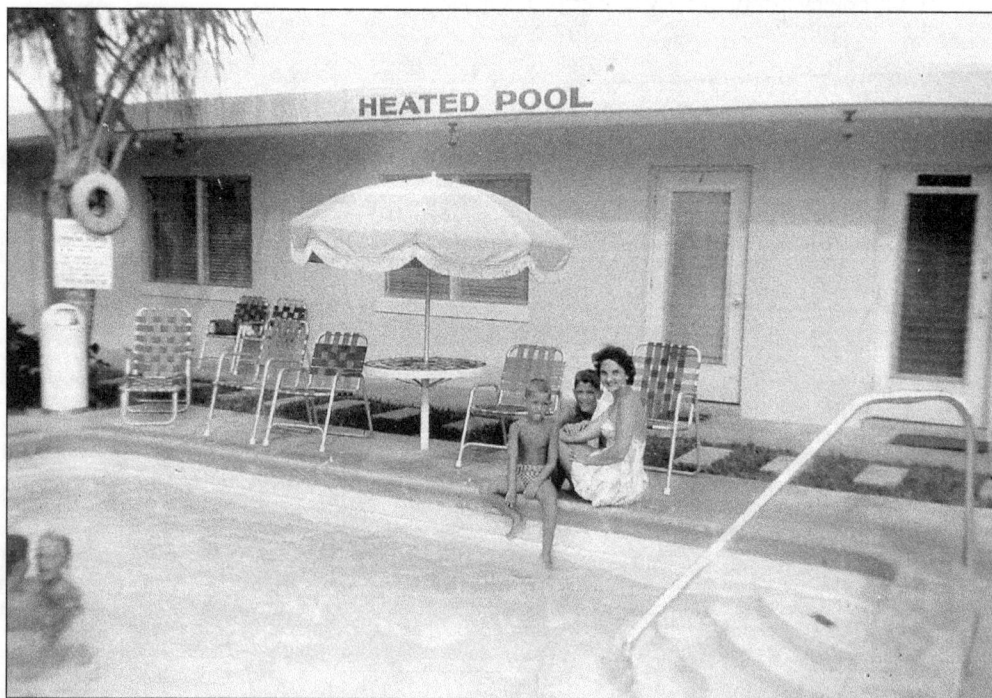

The author (center), his brother Dave, and mother Martha cool off at the Pelican's pool during a summer vacation in 1957.

The Surf, which made its debut in the 1950s, was a standout property sporting the trendy post-war modern look. The gleaming structure quickly gained cachet and helped fuel the resort development boom that would legitimize the city's self-proclaimed status as the "Heart of the Holiday Isles." The Surf is slated to be torn down, despite the protests of local preservationists, to make way for a condo development.

This view through the entryway of the Southwind shows guests enjoying the courtyard. Courtyards were a common motel amenity that offered opportunities for sunning and socializing. The Southwind, which stood at 11700 Gulf Boulevard, has been replaced by condominiums.

One property that has undergone little change over the years is the Arvilla, shown here in the mid-1950s. The property features a spacious courtyard and a shuffleboard court, another popular amenity of the day. The motel advertised "100% air conditioning and TV."

Postcards promoting the Arvilla featured custom-designed artwork showing the motel's proximity—somewhat exaggerated—to local landmarks.

44

This 1952 aerial view of mid-Treasure Island shows the Sea Chest, Edward James, and Tropic Terrace motels lining the beachfront, while property to the east lies undeveloped. Note the width of the beach during this period. (Courtesy of Heritage Village.)

A fresh coat of paint and added amenities—such as beach umbrellas, playground equipment, and shuffleboard courts—gave older cottage-style developments a new lease on life and assured continued patronage from a loyal clientele.

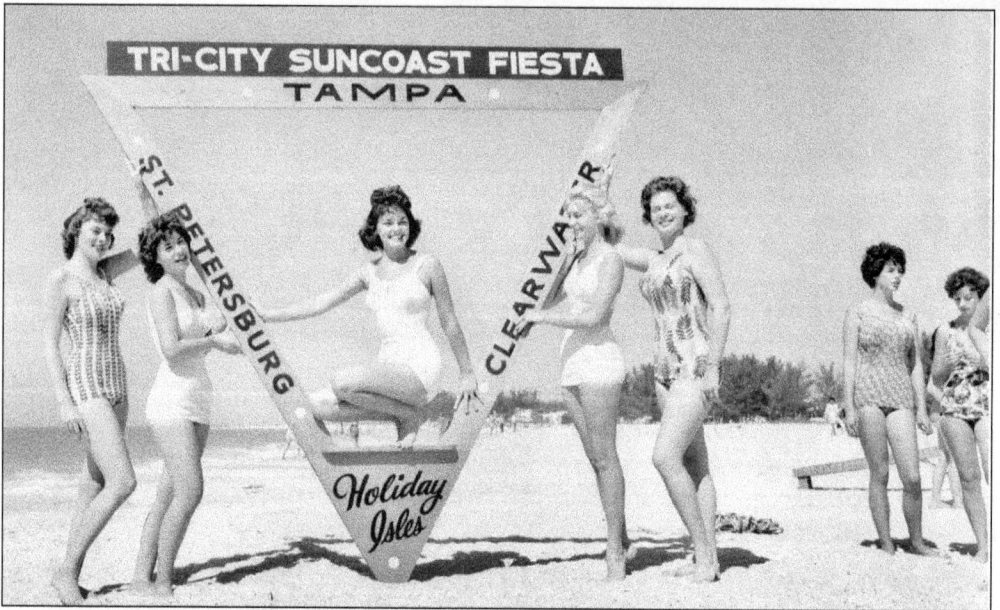

The Tri-City Suncoast Fiesta featured events to promote the Holiday Isles, as the barrier islands comprising the Gulf beaches were called. Here bathing beauties kick off the 1961 festival at Treasure Island. (Courtesy of Florida State Archives.)

Dredging operations brought new housing subdivisions from the depths of Boca Ciega Bay. This 1952 view shows development of Paradise Island getting underway. In the foreground is the first home on Dolphin Drive, while the houses on Treasure Lane, in the background, are ready for landscaping. (Courtesy of Heritage Village.)

Municipal Beach on Treasure Island

The City of St. Petersburg established a municipal beach on Treasure Island in the 1950s. Central Avenue, St. Petersburg's main street, led to the Treasure Island Causeway, giving St. Pete residents easy access to the Gulf Shore. This 1960s view also shows growth of housing developments on the Isle of Palms (center) and Isle of Capri (upper left).

Children play on the wide expanse of the municipal beach, evidence of the family appeal of Tampa Bay's Gulf beaches. The municipal beach and original pavilion are still in operation, continuing to provide a cool respite from city heat.

47

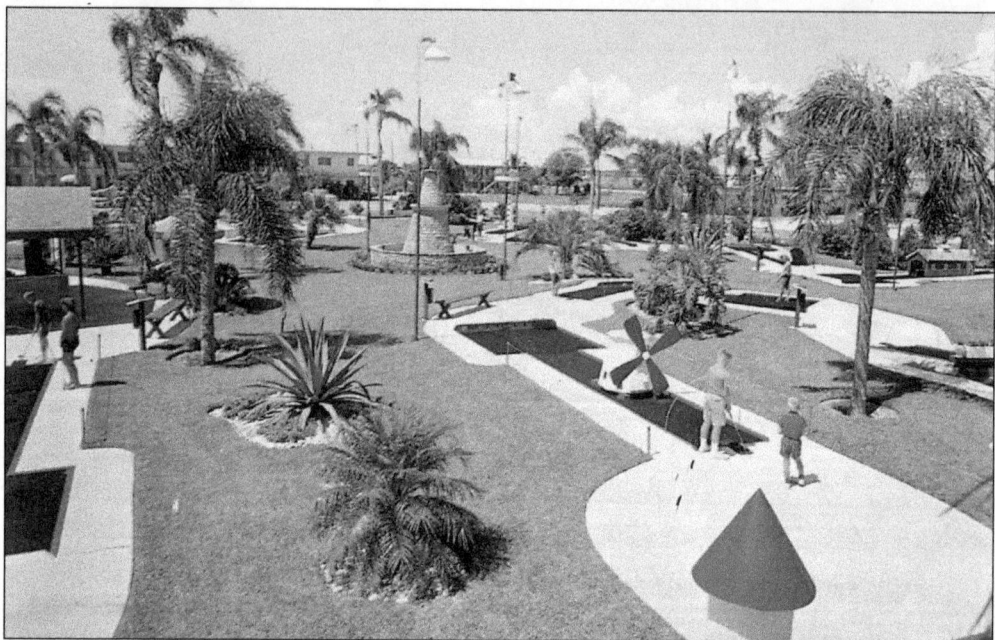

Miniature—or putt-putt—golf, a post-war invention ideally suited to the Florida climate, grew in popularity as a family recreation during the 1950s. Gulf Golf, shown here, is said to be the first miniature golf course in the area. The facility is still in operation at 11605 Gulf Boulevard.

Shops offering seashells of all shapes and sizes and other curiosities of the sea were popular among tourists seeking an authentic vacation souvenir. The Florida Shell Shop, shown here in the 1950s, has been a Treasure Island landmark for almost 50 years. (Courtesy of St. Petersburg Museum of History.)

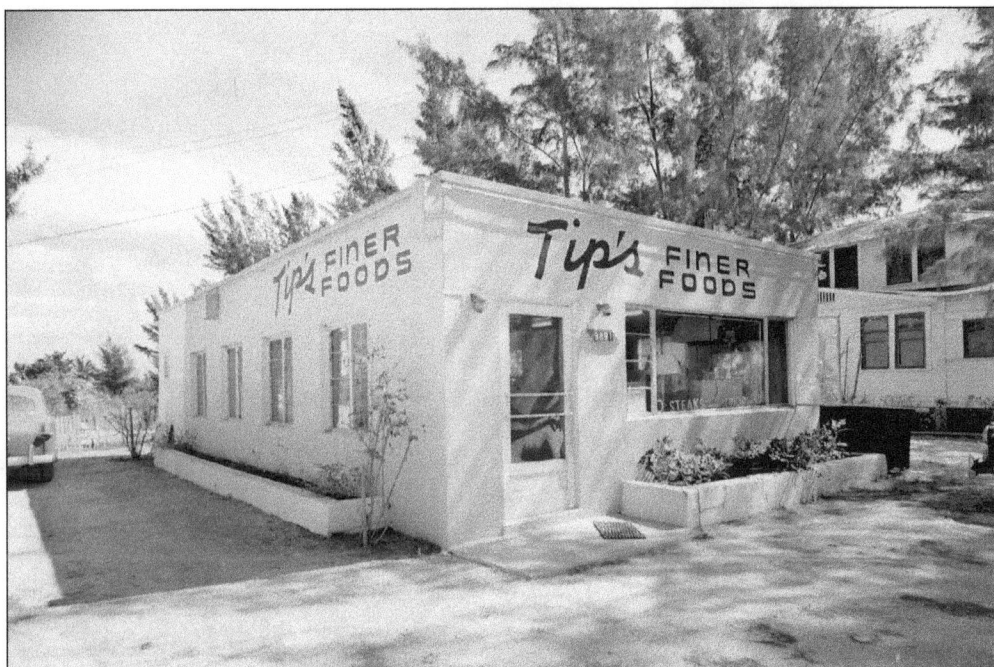

A throwback to pre-war days, neighborhood eateries such as Tip's Finer Foods were gradually replaced by larger, more exotic restaurants and cafeteria chains. Owner Clarence Tippey's restaurant was at 9891 Gulf Boulevard on Sunset Beach.

This 1953 photo shows the nautical-themed bar at the Sunset Playground on Sunset Beach. (Courtesy of Heritage Village.)

Worshipers from the Lutheran Church of the Holy Comforter are shown here celebrating an Easter sunrise service. The tradition of decorating the 30-foot cross with thousands of blooms continues to this day. The church, located on Paradise Island, was one of a number of congregations established on the barrier islands to serve the spiritual needs of the new residents.

Commercial development also took off in Treasure Island during the post-war years. This c. 1960 photo shows the shopping areas near the foot of the causeway with full parking lots. Motels surround the Thunderbird along the beach, and vacant land is becoming scarce.

Four

JOHN'S PASS

John's Pass, created by a major storm in the mid-1800s, has drawn fishermen to its bountiful waters since the earliest days of settlement. The old bridge across the Pass, erected in 1927, became a magnet for anglers who lined its reaches, and fishing-related businesses set up shop along the bridge accesses. This 1950s photo shows the famous Kingfish Seafood Restaurant in its original location, along with the related John's Pass Fish Co. and fishing boats El Capitan and Miss Judy. (Courtesy of Arnold Alloway.)

The old bridge spanned the Pass from an approach just east of the current bridge. The dock for the *El Capitan*, a deep-sea fishing boat, can be seen at the right.

The Gulf waters teemed with game fish, and boats returning after a few hours of deep-sea angling usually displayed a bountiful catch. The *Atlanta*, shown here, was a part of the area's "largest established deep-sea fishing fleet."

Miss Judy, another mainstay of the John's Pass fishing fleet, was operated by Capt. C.O. Fiers from docks next door to Kingfish Restaurant. Fishermen during that era were allowed to sell their catch to local restaurants, and many seafood houses featured shore dinners supplied from the deep-sea boats.

This aerial view shows the old bridge and surrounding area. The Kingfish Seafood Restaurant, John's Pass Fish Co., and other businesses can be spotted along the bridge approach on the Treasure Island side of the bridge (right). On the left are the beginnings of what was to become John's Pass Village.

This earlier photo, taken in 1949, shows only two buildings, a grocery and the VFW, whereas John's Pass Village shops now line old Gulf Boulevard. (Courtesy of Arnold Alloway.)

The John's Pass Village development began as a rather mundane shopping center featuring typical service businesses. The area was promoted in the 1950s and 1960s as "Fish Friendly" John's Pass.

The Marine Arena opened at John's Pass in 1953 and remained a popular tourist venue for over a decade. The attraction was billed as "The West Coast's Largest Attraction" and featured a porpoise tank along with 28 aquariums displaying marine animals. The facility prospered for a number of years before succumbing in 1965 to competition from the larger Aquatarium in St. Petersburg Beach. It enjoyed a brief new life as John's Pass Aquarium after the Aquatarium closed in 1978. (Courtesy of Arnold Alloway.)

Porpoise shows were a main attraction at the Arena, with a pair of dolphins, Patti and Mark, sharing top billing. The animals were the namesakes of Patti and Mark Hubbard, local children whose parents operated Hubbard's Dock at Pass-a-Grille. Patti and Mark are currently executives with the Hubbards' family operations at John's Pass Village. In this photo, Patti the Dolphin leaps from the water to take a fish from her trainer.

Fishermen aboard the *Sea Biscuit*, a smaller boat operating out of John's Pass, display a large catch. The old bridge can be seen in the background. (Courtesy of Heritage Village.)

This later view, taken in 1973, shows the newly completed John's Pass Bridge, with the approach to the old bridge visible on the right. The old approach road now terminates at the former Kingfish Restaurant and is aptly renamed Kingfish Way. (Courtesy of Arnold Alloway.)

Five

MADEIRA BEACH

The beaches' post-war popularity brought rapid growth to the area, and the focus of development moved from St. Petersburg and the mainland to the barrier islands. The city of Madeira Beach was incorporated in 1947, earlier than most of the beach communities. In 1953 when this photo was taken, the business section along Gulf Boulevard and the causeway was being established, and homes were rising rapidly on islands dredged from Boca Ciega Bay. (Courtesy of Heritage Village.)

Billboards along major highways leading south, like this one along U.S. 92, beckoned visitors to "Florida's Fastest Growing Resort City." (Courtesy of Arnold Alloway.)

By 1957, Madeira Beach was already running out of room to grow, and sand was dredged from the bay to create the Crystal Drive, Lillian Drive, and John's Pass Avenue neighborhoods. (Courtesy of Arnold Alloway.)

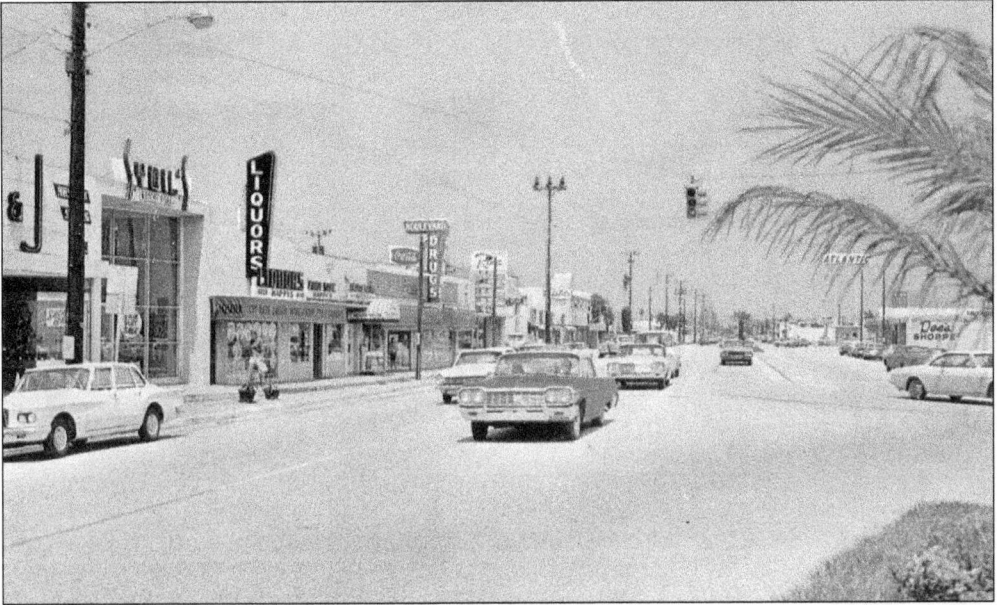

Downtown Madeira Beach spread out from the causeway, along both sides of Gulf Boulevard as shown here, and down Madeira Way.

Businesses along Gulf Boulevard included drug stores, gas stations, clothing outlets, restaurants, and cocktail lounges.

Madeira Way, shown here in the 1950s, remains a busy shopping thoroughfare.

This aerial mid-1960s view shows downtown Madeira Beach lined wall to wall with businesses. To the left, the newly dredged land around today's City Hall is ready for development.

Publix Markets sponsored the opening of a new shopping center located east of the bridge on the north side of the causeway. With the Publix store as anchor, the center quickly filled with tenants. Today an expanded Publix continues to anchor the bustling complex, joined by other prime retailers such as Walgreens, Bealls, Hallmark, and the Sign of the Dolphin Gift Shop. (Courtesy of St. Petersburg Museum of History.)

Guys restaurant occupied space at the eastern end of the center in the 1950s.

ORANGE BLOSSOM GROVES
ONE MILE NORTH OF BAY PINES
LARGO, FLORIDA

ORANGE BLOSSOM GROVES
VISITORS WELCOME
C.O. BUD HUTCHISON   AL REPETTO

Not far from the shopping center, acres of citrus groves offered tourists plenty of Florida's signature fruit. Orange Blossom Groves is still doing business in expanded quarters at the original location on Seminole Boulevard.

The newly organized Madeira Beach Bank, shown here in 1952, was the first bank to incorporate in the city. Bank establishments began to flock to the beaches during the development boom. This building is still standing at the causeway and East Madeira Avenue.

BAY PALMS PARK
Madeira Beach
St. Petersburg, 9la.

Fishing was a big draw to Madeira Beach, as evidenced by this string of beauties taken from the Gulf waters and displayed by residents of Bay Palms trailer park. The park, located on the south side of the causeway just west of the bridge, was the site of Pirates Cove miniature golf course in recent years before being replaced by Snug Harbor condominiums in 2003.

Madeira Beach, Florida   C133

Madeira's wide, sandy beachfront was a big attraction for vacationing families. In this spot, the beach is spacious enough to accommodate playground equipment, and picnickers enjoy the shade of a few Australian pines.

Madeira Beach accommodations in the 1950s and 1960s featured an eclectic mix ranging from motels like the Skyline at 140th Avenue (above) to modest beach cottages like the Sans Souci (below). The Sans Souci was located at 15208 Gulf Boulevard, the site of the Holiday Inn, now being replaced by the Soreno Condominiums. Note the stands of Australian pines that provided the barrier islands with shade cover from the 1920s until freezes in the 1960s and 1980s killed off the exotic species.

The Surf Song Cottages at 12930 Gulf Boulevard, near John's Pass, offered one- and two-bedroom units on a private beach.

This older, two-story frame building offered guests a courtyard area and drive up parking. The Cromwell Arms was located at 14715 Gulf Boulevard.

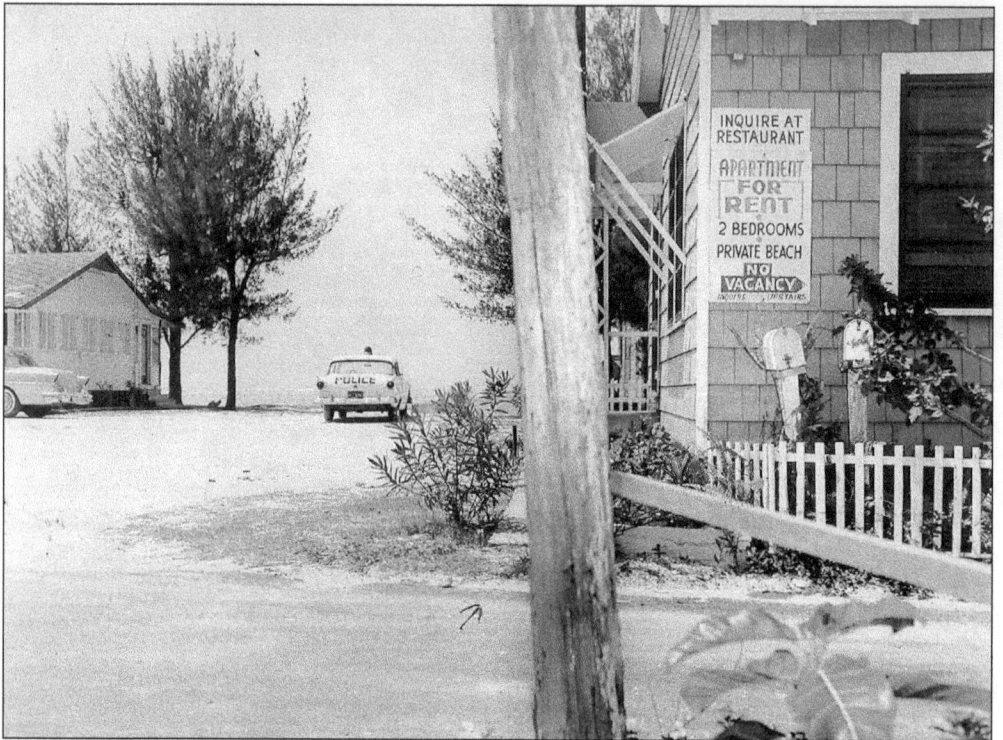

Owners of beach houses, like this dwelling at the end of 131st Avenue, often converted extra space into money-generating tourist quarters. (Courtesy of Arnold Alloway.)

These tires were dumped about 10 miles offshore in the Gulf to create a reef in hopes of attracting fish. According to local fishermen, the ploy worked well. Residents still report seeing an occasional tire or two from the project washed ashore after a storm. (Courtesy of Arnold Alloway.)

Madeira Beach dining choices ranged from plush, exotic establishments to curb-service drive-ins. Near the top of the line was the Kapok Tree Inn, a scaled-down version of the famous Clearwater landmark, which featured an entryway flanked by Greek statues, extensive landscaped grounds, and exotic open-air dining areas. The dining experience was a big hit with tourists, and the Kapok Tree–Madeira flourished until the 1970s, when the Duhme Road property was sold for condo development.

THE FLAMINGO DINING ROOM
14603 Gulf Blvd.
Madeira Beach
St. Petersburg, Florida

The Flamingo Dining Room at 14603 Gulf Boulevard offered more than 50 foods served as a smorgasbord, "cooked and presented in the Scandinavian manner." The restaurant later became the Scandia.

Drive-in restaurants and movies were popular in the 1950s and 1960s, especially with young people. Lindy's Drive-In, located at 15141 Gulf Boulevard, offered curb service from a menu prominently posted over the entrance. Short order foods were available along with fountain sodas, shakes, and sundaes.

The Cajun Diner was imported from New Jersey and opened by George and Pat Shontz on the Madeira Way triangle in 1956. The food was home-style, not Cajun—the original owner, a Mr. Brown, had named the diner in honor of his Cajun wife. The location was later home to the Shontzes' legendary Apple Restaurant and is now Leatherback's Steak House, run by Todd Broaderick. (Courtesy of Patricia Shontz.)

This lighted cross atop the Church by the Sea is a reminder of the original beacon that was held aloft on a 25-foot mast to guide fishermen safely home. The light was kept burning each night until the last fisherman had come in. The church was built over a period of years in the 1940s by the local fishermen, who held weekly fish fries to raise funds for the building materials. (Courtesy of Gulf Beaches Public Library.)

Ladies of the Gulf Beaches Women's Club started the Gulf Beaches Public Library. The city assumed ownership of the modest facility on 140th Avenue in 1950. The current library, located across from City Hall, was built in 1970 at an estimated cost of over $125,000. In this photo, Edyth Mariani, the first librarian, is shown in front of the original building. (Courtesy of Gulf Beaches Public Library.)

Public Works employees set out candles in paper bag luminaries as part of a Christmas celebration in the mid-1960s. (Courtesy of Gulf Beaches Public Library.)

Six

THE REDINGTONS

Including Redington Beach, North Redington Beach, and Redington Shores

America's Longest Resort Beach

For years, the area comprising the Redingtons, including Redington Beach, North Redington Beach, and Redington Shores, was defined by the Tides Hotel and Bath Club, a sprawling resort complex Charles E. Redington built in the mid-1930s to call attention to his lonely stretch of beachfront property. Growth and development followed, as founder Redington predicted, and by the 1960s the area was booming with motels, residences, and service businesses. The Tides Hotel was demolished in 1995 to make way for the Tides Condominiums.

In 1945, the Tides was purchased by Charles Alberding and his partner D.L. Connett and became the showplace of their Alsonette hotel chain. Famous guests willingly went along with promotional stunts staged by Alberding to bring publicity to the hotel. Here Li'l Abner of radio fame is chased by a bevy of attractive models. (Courtesy of Florida State Archives.)

The Bath Club served as the social center of the beaches, and the resort counted as guests such luminaries as Marilyn Monroe and Joe DiMaggio, shown here during a 1961 visit. The resort was also handy to the Yankees' spring training location in St. Petersburg. Other famous guests included Ronald Reagan and filmmaker Alfred Hitchcock. (Courtesy of Heritage Village.)

Actor and Tides guest Tyrone Power autographs the bathing cap of Azalea Queen Jeanne Crow in this *c.* 1950 publicity shot. The onlookers were Webb's City "mermaids." Webb's City in St. Petersburg was touted as "the world's most unusual drugstore." (Courtesy of Florida State Archives.)

Synchronized swimmers display their talents in this 1961 aquatic show held at the Tides's Olympic-sized pool. (Courtesy of Florida State Archives.)

Stunts such as this trapeze act were a common sight at the Tides as owner Charles Alberding pulled out all stops to promote his flagship hotel. (Courtesy of Brian Cocozza.)

Membership in the Tides Bath Club, the only private club in Pinellas County, included prominent area citizens and socialites. A waiting list of up to 20 years existed for the club's 25 exclusive beachfront cabanas. (Courtesy of Brian Cocozza.)

In this 1951 photo, a group of teenagers builds a sandcastle on the Tides beach. Bob Dale, third from left, is currently alumni director of St. Petersburg High School. His parents, Marie and George Foley, were longtime members of the Tides Bath Club. (Courtesy of Bob Dale.)

Corporate and social functions were also a part of the crowded Tides activity calendar. An organist provides musical accompaniment for this gathering. (Courtesy of Brian Cocozza.)

The Tides's success prompted the opening of another prominent resort just down the road. The Glades Hotel, at 17350 Gulf Boulevard in North Redington Beach, was built c. 1950 during the beginning of the area's post-war boom. By 1952, when this photo was taken, land east of the Glades was cleared and ready for development. Creation of new waterfront property by dredging can be seen at the upper right. (Courtesy of Heritage Village.)

The Glades touted "ultra-modern luxury accommodations" and also featured the Evergreen Room for fine dining. In the 1980s, the property was renovated and reopened as the current Grand Shores West timeshare resort. (Courtesy of Heritage Village.)

Like the Tides, the Glades was heavily promoted through advertising, brochures, and local publicity.

Glades recreational amenities included a shuffleboard court, landscaped grounds, beach volleyball, and a heated swimming pool.

This 1955 public relations photo shows the "Swingin' Largo School Band" about to perform around the Glades resort pool. (Courtesy of Largo Library and Largo Historical Society.)

This 1952 aerial view shows the Tides, lower center, the La Playa down the beach to the right, "and other transient and permanent accommodations." The area at the upper right, which was to become the city of Redington Beach the following year, can be seen filling in with single-family homes. (Courtesy of Heritage Village.)

The La Playa Apartment Resort offered spacious one- and two-bedroom apartments, cabanas, and a 300-foot fishing pier.

The Coral Dining Room at the La Playa catered to local residents as well as hotel guests.

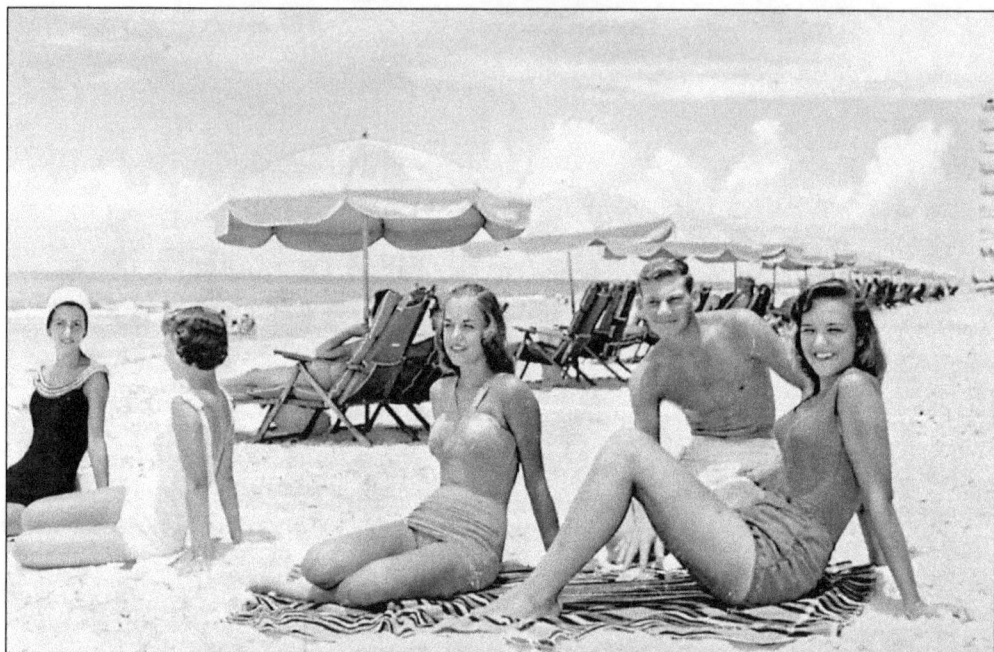

Ed's Beach Service supplied umbrellas in the summer and cabanas in the winter to guests of the La Playa, pictured here, and other Gulf Coast resorts.

This 1960s view looking north over the Redingtons shows the La Playa with fishing pier at lower right, then the high-rise Redington Apartments, now Redington Reef, built in 1958. Just to the north is the Tides Hotel complex.

The Heyer home, shown here in exterior/interior views taken shortly after construction in 1952, is presented as "typical of the high type of residential construction on Redington Beach." Estimated cost of the home was listed as between $50,000 and $60,000. (Courtesy of Heritage Village.)

Parsley's Trailer Park offered bay-front living for full- and part-time residents of more modest means. Parsley's, located in an unincorporated area of Pinellas County surrounded by Redington Shores, has been in operation as a mobile-home park for over 50 years. A mixed-use condo development is now being planned for the property.

Trailers on the Gulf, located at 18200 Gulf Boulevard in Redington Shores, was "St. Petersburg's only trailer park directly on the Gulf of Mexico," according to this card. The complex, now a community park, offered apartments, trailer spaces, and rentals on a private beach with a fishing pier.

In the days before skin cancer concerns, suntan lotion was applied to encourage tanning, and maximum exposure was the goal. This 1950s photo shows Webb's City poster girl Janet Ruth Crockett applying suntan oil while her companion relaxes in the shade of a cabana. (Courtesy of Florida State Archives.)

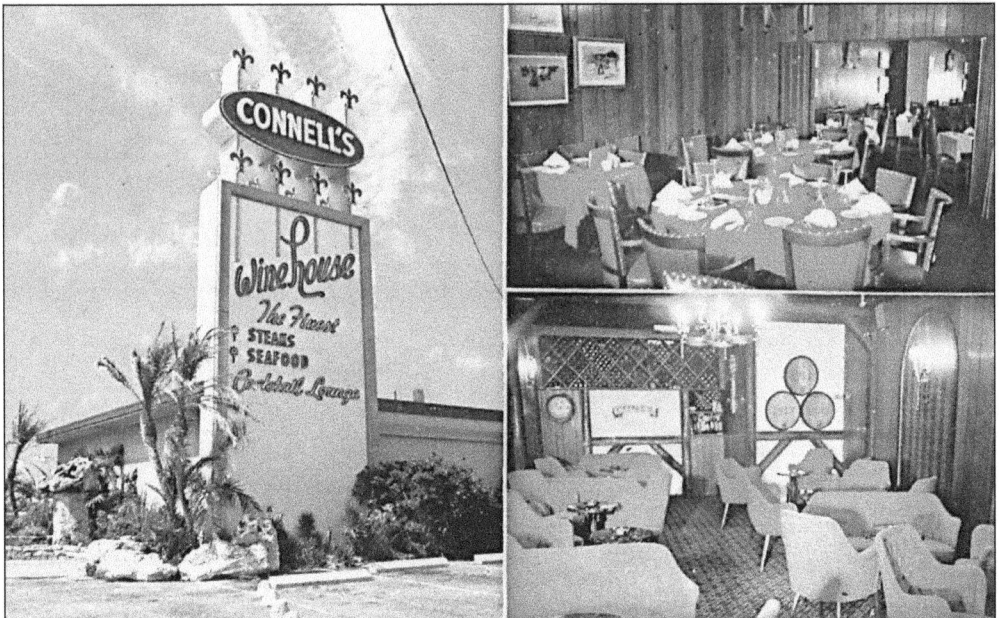

Huge, flashy neon signs vied for attention along the beach strip of the 1950s and 1960s. Connell's Winehouse offered upscale dining specialties, including Knickerbocker Show Award prime meats, double-thick lamb chops, sautéed frog legs, and the original Greek salad. The restaurant, located at Gulf Boulevard and 173rd Avenue across from the Glades Hotel, now operates as the Wine Cellar.

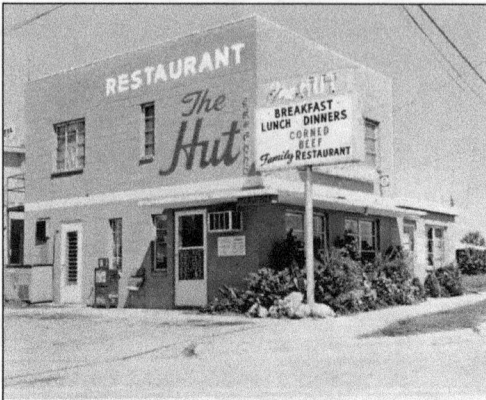

The Hut Family Restaurant and Apartments, located at 17702 Gulf Boulevard, touted itself as "the largest little restaurant on the Holiday Isles." The restaurant was owned and operated by the Dennison family. It is now called Kenny's Korner.

Lilly's Italian Restaurant—a stand-alone, concrete-block, no-frills establishment—featured real Italian spaghetti and offered home cooking, beer, and wine. The eatery, shown here in 1952, stood at 178th and Gulf Boulevard.

Seven

INDIAN ROCKS BEACH
Including Indian Shores

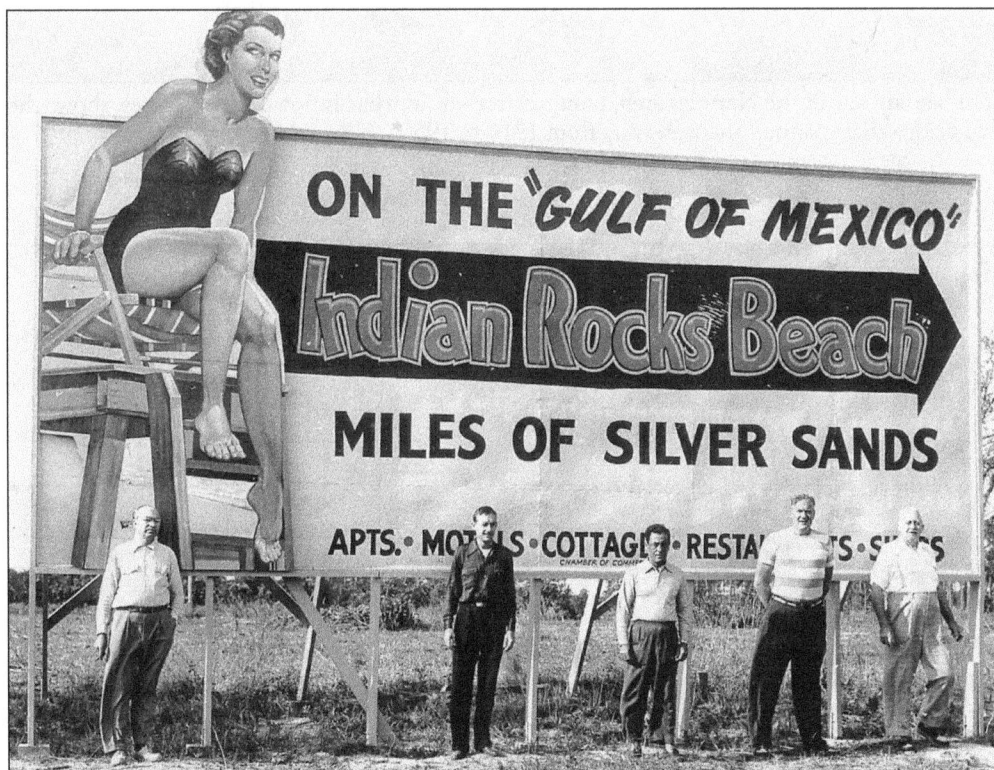

The post–World War II tourist boom was fueled by extensive promotion of the beaches as the place to be. This huge billboard, sponsored by the Chamber of Commerce, pointed the way to the "silver sands" at Indian Rocks Beach. With roots dating back to the 1800s, Indian Rocks, along with Pass-a-Grille and Clearwater, was one of the original beach settlements. The Indian Rocks area included Indian Shores as well as Belleair Beach, Belleair Shore, and parts of Largo across the waterway. The current boundaries were set when the city incorporated in 1955, following an ill-fated attempt in the 1920s. (Courtesy of IRB Historical Museum.)

This aerial view of the Narrows area, looking north from what is now Indian Shores, shows the old bridge that spanned the waterway from 1916 to 1960.

The original bridge, called "Old Rickety," was the first bridge from the mainland to the barrier islands and continued to be a vital connection through the 1950s until it was dismantled in 1960. Through the entire 44 years of use, a bridge tender was required to turn a giant key to swing the bridge open for boat traffic.

Construction of the new Indian Rocks Bridge in 1958, a mile north of the old wooden span, gave tourists an express route to the beach. This bridge, which joined Walsingham Road in Largo to Fifth Avenue in Indian Rocks Beach, was a major impetus for the tourist growth and development surge that followed. (Courtesy of Florida State Archives.)

C-24—Beautiful Indian Rocks Beach, Fla., "On the Gulf of Mexico"

Because of its extensive development as a community of beach homes for vacationing Tampans, Indian Rocks Beach never acquired the "motel row" resort development characteristic of most other areas up and down the barrier island strip. This view shows some of the tourist accommodations along a stretch of Gulf Boulevard, which ran directly along the beach until it was re-routed eastward in the mid-1950s.

Three Indian Rocks churches were born in this American Legion Hut. The Church of the Isles, St. Jerome's Catholic Church, and Calvary Episcopal Church each held services here at some point during the early to mid-1950s while awaiting construction of permanent facilities. (Courtesy of IRB Historical Museum.)

The Indian Rocks Beach community featured an active civic and social scene, with a number of activities enjoying wide popularity. This photo of a 1958 shipwreck party shows, from left to right, Mrs. and Mayor Wallace Dawson dressed as islanders greeting George Manning and his wife Sadie, the sun god and goddess; and Ralph Finke, who was mayor and postmaster in the 1960s, and his wife Avril, who was active in community affairs. (Courtesy of IRB Historical Museum.)

Indian Rocks Beach residents enjoyed a wide range of municipal services and facilities. The city auditorium was built in 1952 with funds raised by the Civic Association. The City purchased the building in 1958 for use as a city hall, offices, and a library. Here, ladies from England's Professional School of Dancing line up for a photo. (Courtesy of IRB Historical Museum.)

Fishing has been a mainstay of the Indian Rocks economy since pioneer days, and it remained a major draw to the area during the post-war tourist boom. Fishing piers jutting out into the Gulf were a common sight along the Indian Rocks Beach shoreline. The famous Big Indian Rocks Fishing Pier, extending out 1,040 feet into the Gulf, dwarfed its competitors as an attraction for anglers.

The Big Indian Rocks Fishing Pier, at Twelfth Avenue, was owned and operated by Charles Moseley, who built it in 1959. Billed as the longest fishing pier in Florida, the structure helped define Indian Rocks Beach as a fisherman's paradise.

These lovely lady anglers lining the pier were part of the 1961 Tri-City Suncoast Fiesta. The pier became a center of social activity in the community and remained so until it was destroyed by the winds and storm surge of Hurricane Elena in September 1985. (Courtesy of Florida State Archives.)

Ten-year-old Bobby Dawson displays a 10-pound cobia caught on the fishing pier the afternoon of August 13, 1962. Bobby and his family had recently moved to Indian Rocks Beach from Oak Ridge, Tennessee. (Courtesy of IRB Historical Museum.)

Cottage accommodations were common along the city's shoreline. Here, tenants pose for a group photo in the sandy front yard of Gooding Manor at 19508 Gulf Boulevard. The Gooding complex also included apartments and a motel. The caption mentions that Gooding Manor was recommended by Duncan Hines, a sign of distinction during the 1950s and 1960s. Hines, in addition to his popular line of cake mixes, published a series of authoritative travel and restaurant guides.

"Guest homes," in which owners rented rooms in their house or adjacent cottage to transient or longer-term visitors, were popular with tourists seeking a more "homey" atmosphere. This also provided a welcome source of income to help pay the mortgage on vacation dwellings.

Dixtom Cottages, at 19015 Gulf Boulevard, offered private screened porches and spacious grounds shaded by the ever-present Australian pines. The towering trees were a dominant feature of the barrier-island landscape from the time of their introduction as an exotic species in the 1920s until they were almost wiped out by hard freezes in the 1960s and 1980s. This area has been made into a nature park by the town of Indian Shores.

The freezes of 1962 and 1984 marked an end to the Australian pines and their ubiquitous presence along Tampa Bay's Gulf beaches. Thousands of trees killed during the cold snap were never replaced due to increased environmental awareness of the threat of alien species to native vegetation. Here the stumps and limbs of dead trees following the 1962 freeze stand as stark sentinels marking the passing of an era. The Big Indian Rocks Pier is in the background. (Courtesy of IRB Historical Museum.)

The Sand Key Cottages touted its location next door to one of the Indian Rocks fishing piers. The mid-1960s setting shows the landscape sans Australian pines following the 1962 freeze.

The Whispering Waters Apartments advertised comfortable one- and two-bedroom apartments. Beach erosion appears to have taken its toll on this locale. Whispering Waters is still doing business at 604 Gulf Boulevard.

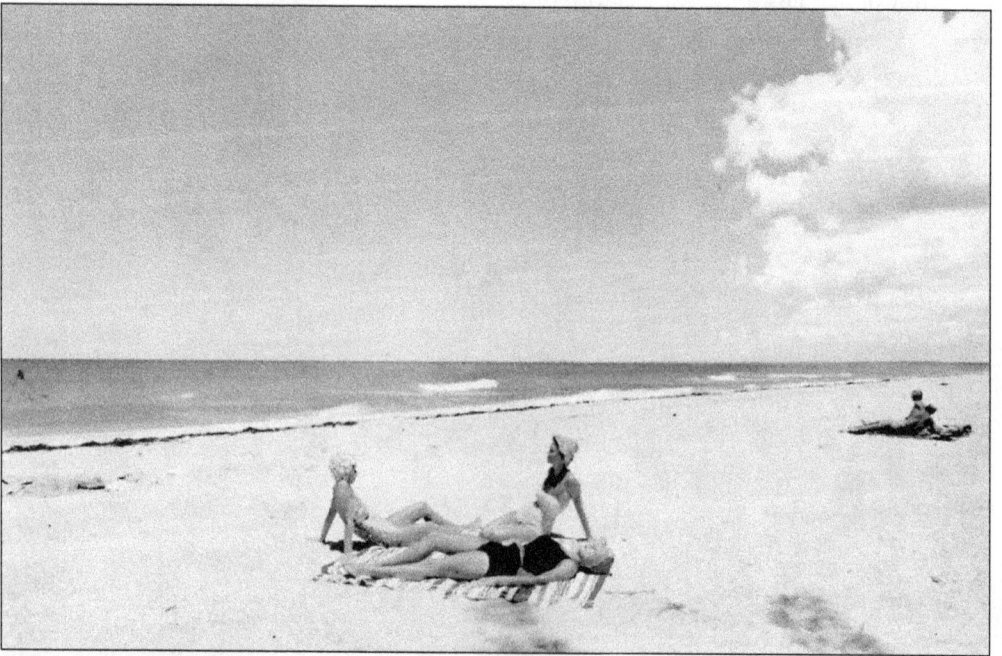

This shot, taken just west of the old bridge, shows the magnificent white sandy beaches that drew tourists to Indian Rocks Beach.

East of Gulf Boulevard, new ranch-style homes were constructed along waterfront property created by dredging the Intracoastal Waterway. These new houses are along the Yacht Basin in the Haven Beach area, which was also home to the venerable Haven Beach Hotel that operated for over 70 years.

This aerial view shows the Haven Beach development, including the hotel (left) shortly after construction of the Walsingham Bridge (top center) in 1958. The Haven Beach Hotel prospered during the post-war boom years but was eventually overshadowed by more modern accommodations in the area and torn down in 1990. (Courtesy of IRB Historical Museum.)

The Haven Beach Hotel, originally the Blue Bird Inn, was built *c.* 1914 as part of the Haven Beach subdivision. The hotel, shown here in the early 1950s, fronted the north end of the Yacht Basin. A 1950s brochure said, "Recreation on our grounds includes shuffleboard courts, outdoor bowling alleys, putting green, horse-shoe pitching, and croquet court." Winter rates started at $15 a week for a hotel room, $35 per week for a cottage. (Courtesy of IRB Historical Museum.)

The Indian Rocks Inn provided visitors with meals and lodging for over 50 years. The inn stood on the beach at the foot of the old bridge, convenient to motorists arriving from the mainland. The structure was remodeled and expanded over the years, and it remained a prominent Indian Rocks Beach hostelry until it was destroyed by fire in 1963. (Courtesy of IRB Historical Museum.)

96

Gulf Boulevard became the main street of Indian Rocks Beach following the war as businesses spread out into available space on the east side of the thoroughfare, from the Narrows north to the Belleair Beach line. (Courtesy of IRB Historical Museum.)

A surge in automobile ownership by a burgeoning middle class after the war brought thousands of tourists to Florida resort areas for the first time. Gas stations to service the many new car owners proliferated along the highways and in tourist spots. Typical of many early service stations, Foerste's offered auto-related services, including a garage and body shop, in addition to pumping gas. Foerste's was located at 405 Gulf Boulevard. (Courtesy of IRB Historical Museum.)

Pueblo Village, opened in 1956 by brothers William and Joseph McNally, was an Indian Rocks Beach institution for years. The property acquired its Spanish Old West look during a 1963 expansion. Looking like it was dropped in from Arizona or New Mexico, the facility quickly became a tourist attraction in its own right. The building, located at 1500 Gulf Boulevard, was torn down in the early 1990s to make way for condos. (Courtesy of IRB Historical Museum.)

Ferman Moodie and his family had living quarters above his drug-and-sundries store at 127 Gulf Boulevard. Moodie's, popular with tourists as well as locals, featured a soda fountain and carried beach wear and sundries along with medicinal products. The building now houses J.D.'s restaurant. (Courtesy of IRB Historical Museum.)

Liberracci the donkey greets customers outside Capt. Joseph Urga's Indian Rocks Restaurant and Bar at 19915 Gulf Boulevard.

Urga, a former sea captain, had this greeting for patrons: "I've traveled all over the world and spent most of my life on the sea. I found a nice sport on Indian Rocks Beach, won't you come and enjoy it with me?" His restaurant became the Hungry Fisherman in later years and is now Fathoms Island Grill.

INDIAN ROCKS PALM GARDENS, INDIAN ROCKS, FLA.
"First In Food – Finest In Atmosphere"
2-G-428

Extensive orange and grapefruit groves covered much of the Indian Rocks area—now part of Largo—on the mainland side of the bay waters. Indian Rocks Fruits, located on Walsingham Road at Oakhurst Road, capitalized on the popularity of citrus by opening the Palm Garden Restaurant in a garden setting adjacent to its retail fruit store.

The Palm Garden Restaurant featured a spacious dining room and outdoor patio where patrons could dine "amidst an atmosphere of tropical splendor."

100

Indian Rocks Fruits promoted its extensive fruit shipping business to tourists wishing to send "an ideal gift of citrus to a friend, relative, or business associate." Note the wooden crates used to protect the fruit during transit. The distinctive labels used by each grower are now sought-after collector's items.

STANDARD FULL BOX
PACKED WITH
STRAIGHT OR MIXED FRUIT
AN IDEAL GIFT TO A FRIEND, RELATIVE OR BUSINESS ASSOCIATE.
THE FAMILY BOX
INDIAN ROCKS FRUITS, Inc. — INDIAN ROCKS, FLA.

Yellow Banks Groves still operates a fruit and gift store on Walsingham Road just east of the bridge. The groves, once located on both sides of Walsingham Road, are long-gone to development. The building pictured here is now located behind the current retail store. Note that Walsingham was a brick road at the time.

The last citrus grove to survive in the Indian Rocks area was J.S. Hill's property on Oakhurst Road. Hill bought his first acreage in 1915 and built a fruit packing plant in 1936. He expanded its operations over several decades, and during the 1950s and 1960s the family owned 60 acres of orange and grapefruit trees. The groves eventually succumbed to residential development, and today the Hill store and packing plant has been renovated into an art gallery.

This early 1960s photo shows Christ the King Lutheran Church surrounded by citrus groves at its new location. The church moved into its current facility on Oakhurst Road on Palm Sunday 1960 after holding services for two years in the Indian Rocks Beach Municipal Building.

Eight

TIKI GARDENS

Tiki Gardens, located in the Indian Rocks area at what is now Indian Shores, was the beaches' nationally acclaimed tourist attraction. The Gardens, which formally opened in 1964, grew from a small gift-shop operation to a multi-acre paradise evoking the South Seas. Tiki Gardens succeeded due to the promotional acumen of owners Frank and Jo Byars in tapping into the public's fascination at the time with South Seas culture. The Gardens prospered over the next decade until overshadowed by megaparks in Orlando and Tampa. It closed in 1985 shortly after being sold by the Byars family to an Australian investor.

The Byarses opened the Signal House gift shop at 196th Avenue and Gulf Boulevard in 1955 as a showcase for Jo Byars's seashell jewelry creations. The shop also sold Polynesian-themed merchandise and local handicrafts. A small garden in the back was the forerunner of Tiki Gardens.

After a devastating fire destroyed the original Signal House in 1964, Frank and Jo Byars decided to capitalize on the Polynesian craze sweeping the nation by turning their property into a South Seas paradise. The Byars hired St. Petersburg architect Robert Lewis Malkin to redesign the Signal House and adjacent Trader Frank's Restaurant and turn the existing gardens into a Polynesian paradise. The new hip-roof gift shop can be viewed here, with the sign at left directing visitors to the Gardens.

A huge sign was a "must" for a major tourist attraction like Tiki Gardens. (Courtesy of Florida State Archives.)

Tiki Gardens' trademarks were the giant Tikis that towered over the grounds. Here a costumed employee begins a reenactment of the Gardens' famous torch lighting ceremony. In the background is one of the gift shops located along the jungle trails.

The torch-lighting ritual, conducted each evening at twilight, was a much-anticipated event at Tiki Gardens. Gardens employees who participated in the ceremony performed under the watchful and meticulous eye of Jo Byars, who closely supervised every aspect of the Gardens' operation.

Gardens visitors walked jungle trails, enjoying attractions along the way such as Monkey Village and Pocco the red macaw, pictured here.

The Garden Chapel, described as a miniature place to worship, was a replica of the Island Chapel of Hawaiian Queens in Hawaii.

The lagoons were a scenic highpoint of a Tiki Gardens visit. This view was taken from the gatehouse veranda.

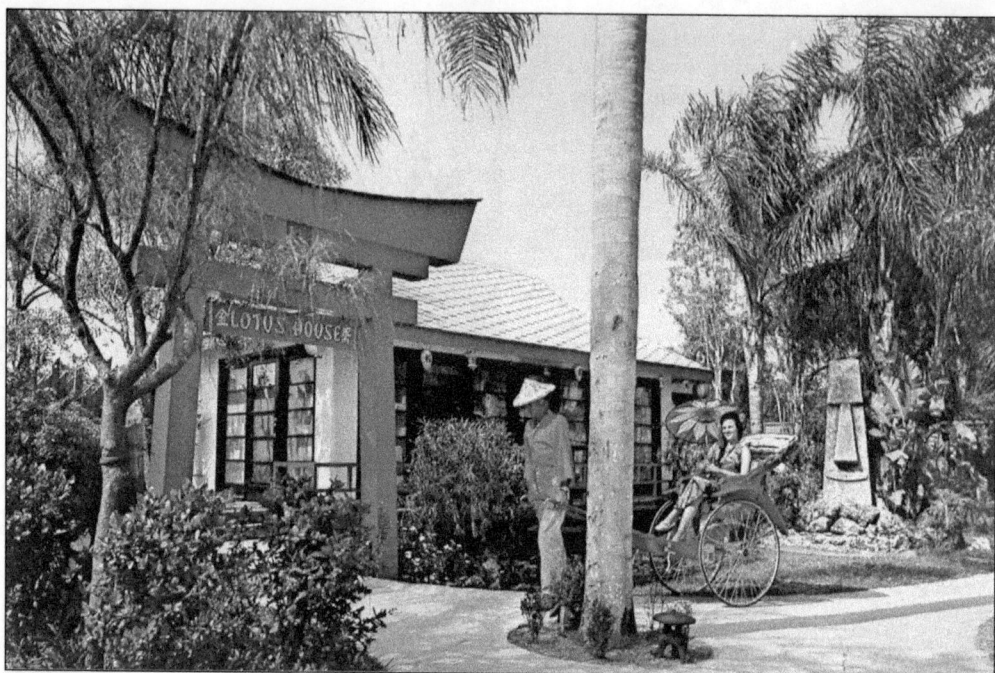

Ten themed gift shops offering exotic selections were located throughout Tiki Gardens. The shops, a testament to the Byarses' merchandising acumen, were the attraction's major revenue generator. Admission to the Gardens was always kept nominal: $1.25 for adults and 75¢ for children. The Lotus House, pictured here, was an oriental grocery store. Rickshaw rides were also available.

The *Tiki* took visitors on a jungle ride along the Intracoastal Waterway.

Nine

BELLEAIR BEACH
Including Sand Key

Construction of the million-dollar Belleair Beach Causeway Bridge in 1949–1950 spurred development on the northern portion of the barrier island Sand Key. The area had served as a practice bombing range during World War II. This photo shows the bridge dedication ceremony held in July 1950. The speaker is Pinellas County commissioner John Chestnut Sr. The tollhouse, where a 25¢ payment was collected from each motorist crossing the bridge, can be spotted in the background. (Courtesy of Heritage Village.)

Congressman-elect Chester B. McMullen was the first motorist to cross the new bridge spanning the Intracoastal Waterway. Here, McMullen hands his quarter toll to Commissioner John Chestnut while district road foreman Walter Waterson looks on. (Courtesy of Heritage Village.)

Island Target Range for Mac Dill Field Bombers at Tampa, Fla.

Bombers from MacDill Air Force Base in Tampa engaged in bombing exercises along the Belleair Beach shoreline during World War II. In later years, spent shells were often found washed up along the beach following storms. (Courtesy of Heritage Village.)

Around-the-clock dredging operations during the late 1940s and 1950s created waterfront property for new residential subdivisions jutting out into the Intracoastal Waterway. By the late 1960s, when this aerial photo was taken, the pattern for Belleair Beach had been set—one-story ranch houses east of Gulf Boulevard with motels (later condos) along the beach. Larger beachfront homes were established in exclusive Belleair Shore, whose northern edge can be seen beginning at the line of palms on the water at the lower left. Sand Key, in the upper background, was undeveloped at this time. (Courtesy of Belleair Beach City Hall.)

This 1969 photo looking east at the northern part of Belleair Beach shows newly created land that would become part of the Belle Isle residential development extending into the bay. The beachfront motel in the lower center is now a part of the Belleair Beach Club. (Courtesy of Belleair Beach City Hall.)

"The Cola" - Belleview Biltmore Hotel - Belleair, Fla.   2-G-542

For years, the Belleview Biltmore Hotel in Belleair ferried its guests by boat across the Intracoastal Waterway to Gulf-front property it owned in Belleair Beach. This photo shows the hotel's boat *Cola* making a run to the beach.

CABANAS AT BELLEVIEW-BILTMORE, BELLEAIR, FLORIDA

One of the earlier structures to be built on the Belleair Beach shoreline was the "Ship" building constructed by the Belleview Biltmore on its beachfront property in 1941. The building, a curious-looking ship replica, offered facilities for hotel guests to change into bathing attire prior to relaxing in one of the Gulf-side cabanas. The Ship was damaged by a storm in 1963 and replaced by the Cabana Club in Sand Key.

The Belleview Biltmore's Cabana Club was located on "a secluded section of white sand beach," according to the description given on this card. The property is still owned by the hotel and is currently the location of the Cabana Club restaurant on Sand Key. (Courtesy of Heritage Village.)

Guests enjoy the patio of the Hohoh Apartments, one of the earliest of the Belleair Beach tourist accommodations. Note the palmetto forests surrounding the property.

113

The "finest in secluded living" was offered at the Surf Apartment Motel, located at 3420 Gulf Boulevard on "150 feet of white sand beach." The structure, now surrounded by condo developments, has been expanded and currently operates as the Nautical Watch motel.

Guests at the Holiday Villas relax in the grassy front yard shaded by palms and Australian pines. The complex featured one- and two-bedroom cottages with screened porches. TV, air conditioning, and tile baths were among the advertised amenities. The Holiday Villas were located at 2740 Gulf Boulevard. Note how close the shoreline is to the seawall.

The northern tip of the barrier island Sand Key, owned by the City of Clearwater, was undeveloped sand when this photo was taken *c.* 1950. Clearwater Pass, which separated Sand Key from Clearwater Beach, was not bridged until 1962. (Courtesy of Heritage Village.)

This 1965 photo shows a rather desolate-looking beach at Sand Key. Wooden groins, built to capture sand and deter erosion, appear to be deteriorating. Dredging equipment can be seen in the background. (Courtesy of Heritage Village.)

By the end of the 1960s, the only pristine beachfront left on the barrier islands was a stretch at the north end of Sand Key owned by the City of Clearwater—but that was not to last. The City sold most of the property for development in the 1980s, and high-rise condos now line all but a small county park at the very northern tip of the key. The original Clearwater Pass Bridge, dedicated on November 30, 1962, can be seen at the top of this picture. (Courtesy of Heritage Village.)

Ten

CLEARWATER BEACH

The city of Clearwater touted its famed wide sandy beach through extensive advertising and promotional events, such as the Fun-'n-Sun Festival, begun in 1954 by the Chamber of Commerce. Held every March to climax the winter season, the event drew crowds of onlookers and plenty of publicity with its extravagant floats, bathing beauties, and marching bands.

Clearwater's big draw was its extensive public beach, long recognized as one of Florida's finest. The jammed parking lots and crowds of sunbathers attest to the area's popularity. This early 1950s photo was taken near the Palm Pavilion. The Clearwater Beach Hotel can be spotted in the background.

The Memorial Causeway Bridge provided easy access to the sugar-white sands of Clearwater Beach. The bridge was also a favorite with anglers who often brought in prize catches of snapper, grouper, pompano, and other tasty saltwater species from the bay waters.

Clearwater Beach in the 1950s featured mostly cottage-type development amid open land and stands of Australian pine. The areas in the upper right, which were to become the site of the Island Estates subdivision, were mangrove islands at this time. Parking space along South Gulfview Boulevard already appears to be at a premium.

The same view, taken in the early 1960s, shows rows of ranch-style homes constructed along the fingers of land reaching into the bay, and motels replacing many of the older wood-frame structures along Gulfview. Motels also now line the previously vacant land to the east along newly created Coronado and Hamden Drives.

This view of Clearwater Beach shows the pier before its extension in the early 1960s.

These unique reclining wicker cabanas were a popular beach accessory available at Rockaway Pavilion, now Frenchy's Rockaway Grill. Palm Pavilion is in the background.

120

The famous Pier Pavilion Pool, shown here c. 1960, played host to top local and regional swimming events. This photo shows the Florida Junior Olympic Swimming Championship finals.

The enduring Palm Pavilion, established in 1926, is the last of the original bathhouse pavilions to survive on Clearwater Beach. The facility currently serves as an informal restaurant-bar. During the 1960s, when this photo was taken, the Palm Pavilion still offered bathhouse facilities along with a snack bar and beachwear shop.

121

Bathing beauties taking part in the 1961 Tri-City Suncoast Fiesta take a run on the beach past the Palm Pavilion. (Courtesy of Florida State Archives.)

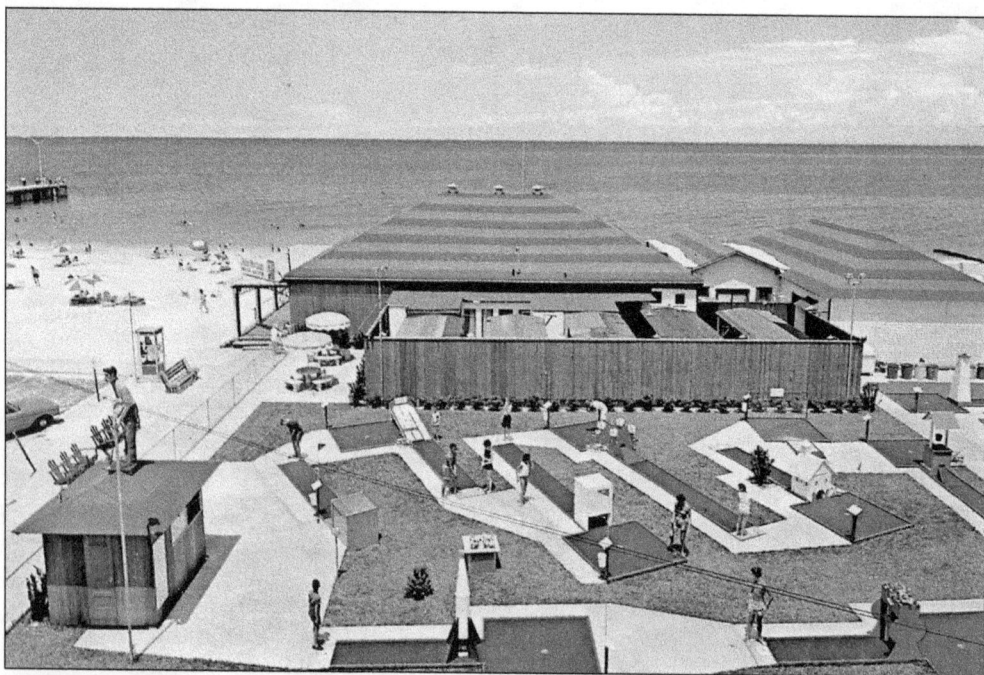

Major renovations to the Palm Pavilion in 1968 included removal of most of the changing rooms to make way for the miniature golf course pictured here.

The Sea Shell, with its distinctive octagonal dome shape, was another Clearwater Beach landmark, dating to the 1930s. Originally it was the Joyland Silver Dome, then it became a clubhouse for the adjacent trailer park, which can be seen here on the left. The structure became a hotel in 1948 when a second floor was added.

This view of the Sea Shell Hotel shows an updated façade with shingles and picture windows. The building was demolished in 1972 to make way for the Clearwater Beach Holiday Inn, which is now the Hilton.

Clearwater Beach Marina

The Clearwater Marina and Yacht Basin was the center of the area's recreational boating and deep-sea fishing fleet. The two-story building at right, which housed the Sea-orama attraction in the 1950s, is now primarily shops. In the foreground is the Port Vue Motel, which still stands at the edge of the marina on Coronado Drive.

This sweeping aerial view shows the marina in the lower foreground; the Pier Pavilion, Olympic swimming pool, and entrance to the pier to the left; shopping areas and motels in the upper portion of the picture; and the causeway entrance in pre-roundabout days on the right. The distinctive Howard Johnson's, which stood at the causeway entrance to the island, can also be seen. The landmark Sea Shell is visible among the Australian pines on the beach.

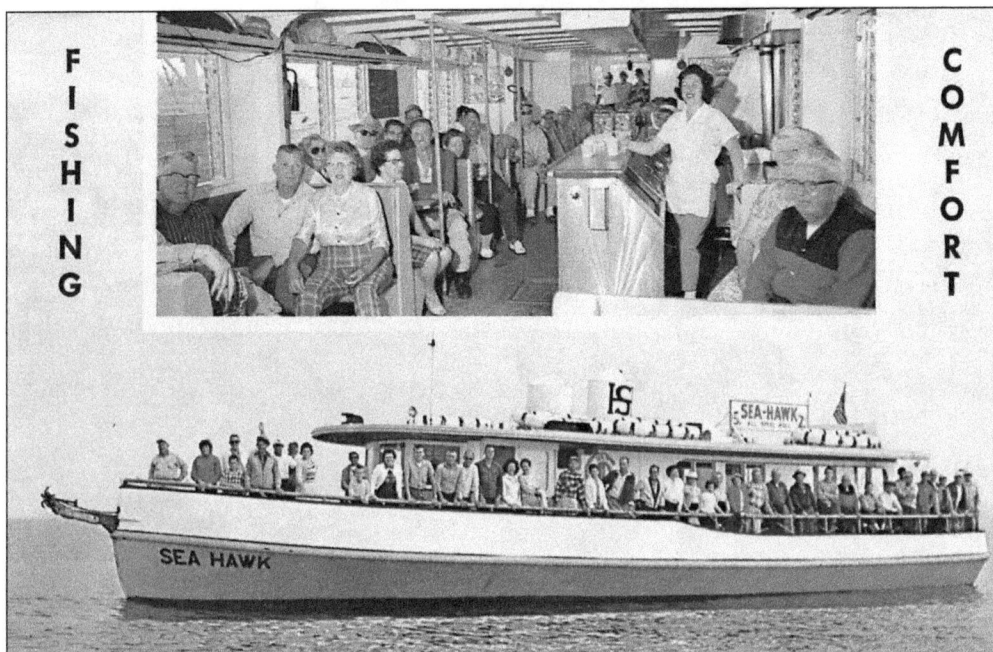

F
I
S
H
I
N
G

C
O
M
F
O
R
T

Deep-sea fishing was a popular activity for Clearwater Beach tourists. Boats headed out daily to the Gulf packed with anglers who often returned loaded down with their catch from the teeming waters. The *Sea Hawk*, pictured here, featured the latest in depth recorders and fish finders. Mr. and Mrs. Pete Doucas owned the boat, which was captained by Mickey Couch.

This southerly view of the Clearwater Pass Bridge, a toll bridge, was taken in 1965 from the location of the long-time Fisherman's Wharf Restaurant, now Leverock's Restaurant on the south end of Clearwater Beach. (Courtesy of Florida State Archives.)

125

The Clearwater Beach Hotel was constructed in 1920 during the original tourist boom and was rebuilt in the 1970s. Guests appear to be enjoying the hotel's spacious grounds in this c. 1960s photo.

The dining room of the Clearwater Beach Hotel, shown here in the 1950s, was a popular rendezvous spot over the years for guests and locals alike to gather for gourmet cuisine served in a classic, congenial setting.

The Glass House, at 229 Gulfview Boulevard, is typical of the smaller motel properties built during Clearwater Beach's 1950s motel construction boom. The structure is one of the surviving mom-and-pop motels that once dominated in Clearwater Beach. It is currently slated for demolition to make way for a major condo development in the area.

This shot from the late 1960s shows the large sandy beach surrounding Pier 60, which has been largely preserved today. The high-rise building in the background, originally Mandalay Shores and now the Regatta Beach Club, signals the beginning of the condo age. (Courtesy of Florida State Archives.)

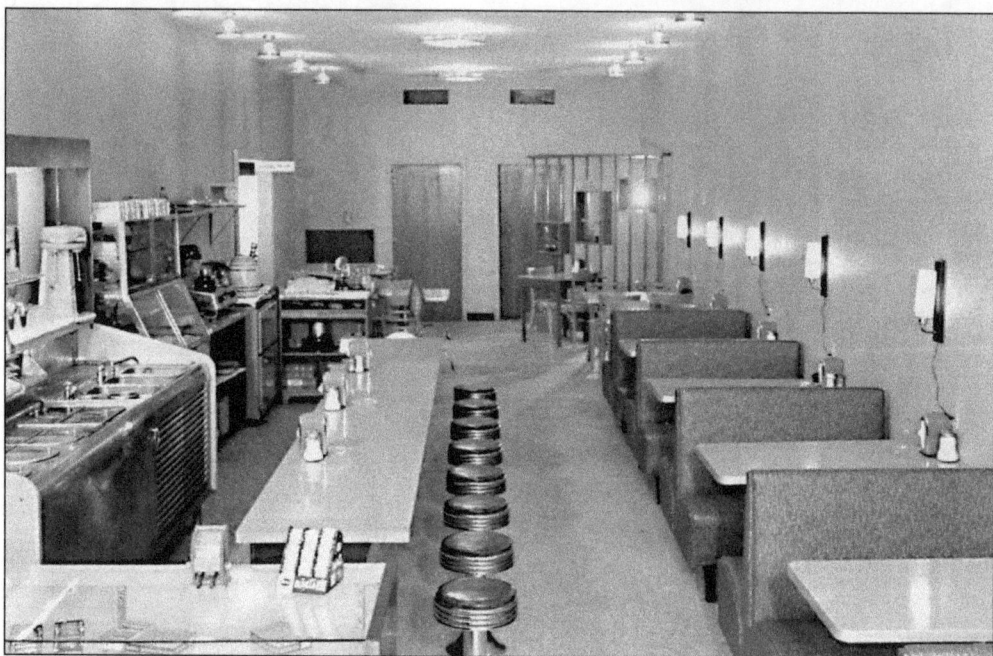

Diner-style restaurants offering a choice of booths, tables, or counter service were a popular dining option in the 1950s and 1960s. The Blue Gulf Restaurant at 387 Mandalay, pictured here, advertised "real Italian food" and "the most tasty pies baked in our own kitchen."

Heilman's Beachcomber remains a Clearwater Beach institution to this day. The restaurant was drawing crowds for its "famous 'back-to-the-farm' fried chicken dinner" in 1954. Air conditioning, a novel and much appreciated amenity during the hot humid summer, was touted with a "Cool Inside" sign fashioned with icicles. Note the cooling tower on the roof.

128

www.ingramcontent.com/pod-product-compliance
Lightning Source LLC
Chambersburg PA
CBHW050601110426
42813CB00008B/2423